Louise Muhdi

Understanding Crowdsourcing - the process and the contributors

Louise Muhdi

Understanding Crowdsourcing - the process and the contributors

Based on the doctoral dissertation "Open Innovation and Collaboration for Innovation", Dr. Louise Muhdi, ETHZ, 2011.

Südwestdeutscher Verlag für Hochschulschriften

Impressum/Imprint (nur für Deutschland/only for Germany)
Bibliografische Information der Deutschen Nationalbibliothek: Die Deutsche Nationalbibliothek verzeichnet diese Publikation in der Deutschen Nationalbibliografie; detaillierte bibliografische Daten sind im Internet über http://dnb.d-nb.de abrufbar.
Alle in diesem Buch genannten Marken und Produktnamen unterliegen warenzeichen-, marken- oder patentrechtlichem Schutz bzw. sind Warenzeichen oder eingetragene Warenzeichen der jeweiligen Inhaber. Die Wiedergabe von Marken, Produktnamen, Gebrauchsnamen, Handelsnamen, Warenbezeichnungen u.s.w. in diesem Werk berechtigt auch ohne besondere Kennzeichnung nicht zu der Annahme, dass solche Namen im Sinne der Warenzeichen- und Markenschutzgesetzgebung als frei zu betrachten wären und daher von jedermann benutzt werden dürften.

Coverbild: www.ingimage.com

Verlag: Südwestdeutscher Verlag für Hochschulschriften GmbH & Co. KG
Heinrich-Böcking-Str. 6-8, 66121 Saarbrücken, Deutschland
Telefon +49 681 37 20 271-1, Telefax +49 681 37 20 271-0
Email: info@svh-verlag.de

Approved by: Zürich, ETH Zürich, Diss., 2011

Herstellung in Deutschland:
Schaltungsdienst Lange o.H.G., Berlin
Books on Demand GmbH, Norderstedt
Reha GmbH, Saarbrücken
Amazon Distribution GmbH, Leipzig
ISBN: 978-3-8381-2876-4

Imprint (only for USA, GB)
Bibliographic information published by the Deutsche Nationalbibliothek: The Deutsche Nationalbibliothek lists this publication in the Deutsche Nationalbibliografie; detailed bibliographic data are available in the Internet at http://dnb.d-nb.de.
Any brand names and product names mentioned in this book are subject to trademark, brand or patent protection and are trademarks or registered trademarks of their respective holders. The use of brand names, product names, common names, trade names, product descriptions etc. even without a particular marking in this works is in no way to be construed to mean that such names may be regarded as unrestricted in respect of trademark and brand protection legislation and could thus be used by anyone.

Cover image: www.ingimage.com

Publisher: Südwestdeutscher Verlag für Hochschulschriften GmbH & Co. KG
Heinrich-Böcking-Str. 6-8, 66121 Saarbrücken, Germany
Phone +49 681 37 20 271-1, Fax +49 681 37 20 271-0
Email: info@svh-verlag.de

Printed in the U.S.A.
Printed in the U.K. by (see last page)
ISBN: 978-3-8381-2876-4

Copyright © 2012 by the author and Südwestdeutscher Verlag für Hochschulschriften GmbH & Co. KG and licensors
All rights reserved. Saarbrücken 2012

If you want to build a ship, don't drum up people together to collect wood and don't assign them tasks and work, but rather teach them to long for the endless immensity of the sea.

Antoine de Saint-Exupery (1900-1944)

DEDICATION

I dedicate my doctoral dissertation to my wonderful daughter Amelia Muhdi, who is and always will be the light of my life.

ACKNOWLEDGEMENTS

I feel fortunate to have been given the opportunity to conduct research at the Chair of Technology and Innovation Management at the Swiss Federal Institute of Technology Zurich (ETHZ) the past three years. For me this time has been most rewarding, enjoyable and has permitted me to strengthen my knowledge in the fields of management and economics.

I would like to thank Prof. Dr. Roman Boutellier for giving me the opportunity to carry out my PhD studies as well as his trust, valuable insight and patience. Also I am immensely grateful to Prof. Dr. Elgar Fleisch for being my co-supervisor.

The most enjoyable and valuable time during my dissertation is the time spent with my colleagues at the chair at the ETH which have as well supported me throughout the process.

Inhaltsverzeichnis

Abstract	5
Zusammenfassung	7
1. Introduction	9
1.1. Open Innovation models	10
1.1.1. Distributed Innovation	10
1.1.2. Open Innovation	12
1.2. Innovation-related online communities	14
1.3. Crowdsourcing	16
1.4. Open Innovation in the context of adoption of novel technologies	18
2. Aim of Research and Research Questions	20
3. Research Methodology	21
3.1. The intermediary-mediated Crowdsourcing process	21
3.1.1. Case study and Crowdsourcing intermediary selection	22
3.1.2. Data sources	23
3.1.3. Project details	25
3.2. Motivation factors of community members in Crowdsourcing	25
3.2.1. Case studies	25
3.2.2. Data sources and project details	26
3.3. Application of Open Innovation approaches	27
4. Key findings	27
4.1. The Crowdsourcing process	27
4.2. Motivation factors important for members' participation and contribution in innovation-related online communities.	29
5. Implications for Further Research	32
6. Articles and summaries	34
6.1. The Crowdsourcing process: an intermediary mediated idea generation approach in the early phase of innovation.	36
6.2. Crowdsourcing for "Kiosk of the Future" – A Retail Store Case Study	38
6.3. Motivational factors affecting participation and contribution of members in two different Swiss innovation communities	40
7. References	42
8. Appendix	47
8.1. List of Interviews	47
8.2. Copies of publications	52
8.2.1. The Crowdsourcing process: an intermediary mediated idea generation approach in the early phase of innovation	52
8.2.2. Crowdsourcing for "Kiosk of the Future" - A Retail Store Case Study	81
8.2.3. Motivational factors affecting participation and contribution of members in two different Swiss innovation communities	100

Abstract

In recent years, there has been a growing interest in the Open Innovation phenomena by academics and practitioners alike. In particular, an ever growing number of companies view Open Innovation practices as a way to increase the efficiency and effectiveness of their innovation processes. Till date, a large number of companies from different industries such as design, consumer goods and the chemical industry have successfully utilized different Open Innovation approaches to enrich their internal innovation processes. However, the shift to Open Innovation and the implementation of Open Innovation practices has generally been difficult for companies around the globe. Despite its immense popularity Open Innovation remains a rather young academic discipline in which academic framework and theories still need to be refined and elaborated on. Today, there is a growing need to understand and differentiate different aspects of Open Innovation such as the different approaches: i.e. how, where and for which purpose they can be successfully applied and managed as a tool within innovation management in order to optimally achieve internal goals or improve results.

This research has increased the understanding of several aspects of the Open Innovation phenomena and made several contributions to current literature. Firstly and based on longitudinal data analysis, five important phases of the intermediary-mediated Crowdsourcing process were identified and described. Moreover, important issues and tasks within each phase, which should be considered when engaging in a Crowdsourcing project, were thoroughly discussed. Secondly, the understanding of members' motivation to participate in and thus contribute to innovation related communities has been improved. In this context two innovation related communities, i.e. a Swiss innovation intermediary community and an internal innovation community of a private company, were investigated and described. Third, and by means of various case studies this research has illustrated how Open Innovation practices are relevant in the context of technology adoption.

Business professionals can utilize the insights gained during the course of this research to improve their understanding of the intermediary-mediated and virtual Crowdsourcing process. In-depth understanding of the different phases and their associated tasks of the Crowdsourcing process can help improve the effective application of Crowdsourcing for idea generation as well as support decision making. The findings can assist companies to optimally integrate Crowdsourcing in an early stage of their innovation processes. Furthermore, they have practical implications for managing innovation-related online communities. Knowing the difference between an intermediary innovation community and an internal innovation community can be valuable knowledge for a company deciding whether to create an internal community or to make use of existing innovation communities (which are usually fostered by intermediaries). Moreover, understanding the factors which motivate individuals to participate in and contribute to innovation communities can help anyone involved with Crowdsourcing to create more motivating environments to enhance collective innovation.

The research methodology used includes a thorough literature research and multiple case studies. Face-to-face interviews and teleconferences with more than 60 interview partners working in companies from different industries as well as by various e-surveys with a large numbers of individuals were conducted. The results of this research project have been published in 10 articles, addressing scientists and practitioners alike.

Zusammenfassung

In den letzten Jahren haben sich sowohl Akademiker als auch Manager vermehrt mit dem Phänomen Open Innovation auseinandergesetzt. Eine setzt wachsende Zahl von Firmen erwägen die Nutzung von Open Innovation Ansätzen, um die Effizienz und Effektivität ihres eigenen Innovationsprozesses zu steigern. Bis heute haben bereits zahlreiche Unternehmen aus unterschiedlichsten Branchen wie Design, Konsumgüter oder der chemischen Industrie, verschiedene Open Innovation Tools zur Bereicherung interner Innovationen erfolgreich eingesetzt. Der Übergang von traditionellen Innovationsansätzen zu Open Innovation sowie die Implementierung der Open Innovation Ansätze gestalten sich allerding als schwierig. Trotz hoher Popularität in den letzten Jahren, bleibt Open Innovation eine relativ junge akademische Disziplin in welcher Theorien und Rahmenbedingungen immer noch weiterentwickelt werden müssen. So steht das Verständnis verschiedener Open Innovation Aspekte im Zentrum der hier vorliegenden akademischer Forschung. Es stellt sich die Frage wie Open Innovation Methoden erfolgreich als Innovations Managament Tools angewandt und gemanagt werden können.

Die vorliegende Forschungsarbeit hat das Verständnis verschiedener Aspekte des Open Innovation Phänomens erhöht und hat wichtige Beiträge zur aktuellen Literatur gemacht. In einem ersten Schritt und basierend auf einer longitudinalen Datenanalyse wurden fünf Phasen des intermediären Crowdsourcings identifiziert. Zudem wurden wichtige Probleme und Herausforderungen innerhalb jeder Phase, welche in Crowdsourcing Projekten berücksichtigt werden müssen, ausführlich diskutiert. In einem zweiten Schritt wurde das Verständnis der Motivationsfaktoren, welche die Beteiligung der Mitglieder beeinflusst, verbessert. In diesem Kontext wurden Gemeinsamkeiten und Unterschiede von zwei Communities, eine Schweizer intermediäre Innovationscommunty und eine firmeninterne Innovationscommunity, erforscht. Schliesslich hat diese Forschung mittels verschiedener Fall Beispiele die

Relevanz von Open Innovation Ansätzen im Kontext der Technologieadaption gezeigt.

Praktiker können die in dieser Forschung gewonnenen Erkenntnisse nutzen, um ihr Verständnis des intermediären und virtuellen Crowdsourcing Prozesses zu erhöhen. Vertieftes Verständnis der verschiedenen Phasen samt der Vorteile und Grenzen des Crowdsourcing Prozesses kann dessen Anwendung zur Ideengenerierung verbessern und auch die interne Entscheidungsfindung unterstützen. Die Erkenntnisse können Firmen helfen, Crowdsourcing in einem frühen Stadium des internen Innovationsprozesses optimal zu integrieren. Zusätzlich ergeben sich aus der Forschung praktische Hinweise zum Management von innovationsbezogenen Online Communities. Kenntnisse der Unterschiede zwischen einer intermediären Innovationscommunity und einer internen Innovationscommunity ist für Firmen hilfreich, welche vor dem Entscheid stehen, eine interne Community anzusprechen oder auf eine externe Innovationscommunity eines Open Innovations-Intermediären zuzugreifen. Die Kenntnis von Faktoren, welche zur Teilnahme in Innovationscommunities motivieren, unterstützen ausserdem Unternehmen beim Aufbau einer innovationsfreundlichen Umgebung.

Die Forschungsmethodologie beinhaltet eine gründliche Literaturrecherche und eine Vielzahl von Fall Beispiele, deren Daten mittels persönlicher und telefonischer Interviews mit über 60 Personen aus verschiedenen Industrien sowie aus verschiedenen e-surveys erhoben wurden. Basiert auf identifizierten Mustern und erfolgreichen Praktiken wurden Übersichten und Vorschläge herausgearbeitet. Die Forschungsresultate wurden in 11 Artikeln publiziert, welche sowohl Wissenschaftler als auch Praktiker ansprechen.

> Innovation is not the product of logical thought, although the result is tied to logical structure.
>
> Albert Einstein (1879-1955)

1. Introduction

Joseph Schumpeter, 1883-1950, identified innovation as the critical dimension of economic change and argued that economic change revolves around innovation. In other words, innovations are responsible for the continuous reformation of industries. In his 1927 paper The Explanation of the Business Cycle (Schumpeter, 1927) and in his seminal work Capitalism, Socialism and Democracy (Schumpeter, 1943), Schumpeter suggested a business cycle theory that emphasizes innovation and entrepreneurship (Figure 1). His work was the first to combine the four business cycles previously described by Kitchin, Juglar, Kuznets and Kondratieff into a single model where these would form a large composite wave.

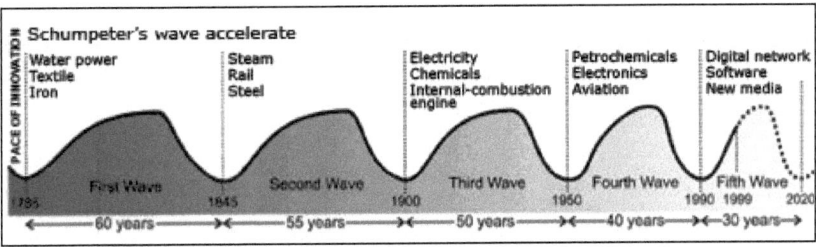

Figure 1 The Schumpeterian cycle of innovation and entrepreneurship (according to Schumpeter, 1927,1943).

The importance of innovation in the creation and maintenance of competitive advantages for companies is a long discussed topic in literature (Brown and Eisenhardt, 1995, Cooper, 2000, Motwani et al., 1999, Hurley, 1998). Already in his 1986 book on management frontiers (Drucker, 1986), Peter Drucker observed that it is the innovative companies which are capable to abandon the products before competitors make them obsolete. Today, it is generally agreed that there is a positive relation between innovation and company performance (Han et al., 1998, Hurley, 1998, Achilladelis and Antonakis, 2001).

Innovations can be incremental or radical and different types of innovations have been identified and described in a large body of literature, e.g. product, service, process, organizational and marketing innovations (Boer and During, 2001, North and Smallbone, 2000, Han et al., 1998). Even though, luck and coincidence still are believed to play a role in the emergence of innovations, various studies have shown that the application of appropriate instruments and processes along with an innovation conscious management style (Thamhain, 2003) and a strong innovation culture (Dombrowski et al., 2007, de Brentani, 2001) can increase the success of innovations in companies.

1.1. Open Innovation models

Several Open Innovation models have been described in literature and act as the theoretical basis of this research.

1.1.1. Distributed Innovation

Innovation in the past often seems to have been dominated by elites – the "wealthy gentlemen tinkerers" who had privileged access to money, information and markets. However, in his book A culture of Improvement: Technology and the Western Millenium (Friedel, 2007) Robert Friedel shows how countless small efforts by different individuals, from all rungs of society's ladder, contributed to the advances that we enjoy today in the post-modern and post-industrial societies.

In a company context, it has long been assumed that product innovations are typically developed by in-house research and development (R&D) departments of product manufacturers. However, it now appears that this basic assumption is often incorrect. During the last decade the propensity to cooperate beyond corporate boundaries, customarily join with others to develop innovations cooperatively or incorporate external knowledge into internal innovations has increased within most companies. In his book Sources of Innovation (von Hippel, 1988) Eric Von Hippel introduced a new model of innovation which is today known as the model of distributed innovation. He pointed out that the manufacturer-as-innovator assumption is wrong and pointed out the need for a new way to categorize innovators. According to Von Hippel the sources of innovation are distributed and can vary between different stakeholders such as users, suppliers, manufacturers, distributors or others. Furthermore, expected rents and economic rationality can predict the likely source of innovation. If a company manages to understand its source of innovation it will most likely be able to undertake the needed internal modification in view to improve its internal innovation process. Additionally, Von Hippel drew attention to the importance of Lead Users in generating commercially promising innovations. The ability to exploit external knowledge and to master the process of harnessing the distributed creative potential is a critical component of innovative capabilities and has been shown to depend on the company's absorptive capacity (Cohen and Levinthal, 1990).

1.1.2. Open Innovation

As industries are becoming more knowledge based, companies are increasingly turning to Open Innovation business models to keep a step ahead of competing innovators. The term Open Innovation was first promoted by Henry Chesbrough in his book Open Innovation: The new imperative for creating and profiting from technology (Chesbrough, 2003b). The Open Innovation phenomena describes the increase in the openness of organizations towards their environment and the utilization of targeted inflows and outflows of knowledge in order to accelerate internal innovation, and expand the markets for external use of innovation, respectively (Chesbrough, 2006). According to Chesbrough (Chesbrough, 2003a, Chesbrough et al., 2006) R&D is an open system in the paradigm of Open Innovation. Ideas are generated both inside and outside the focal firm. Furthermore, external knowledge plays the same role as internal knowledge and is not just useful or supplemental as described in earlier theories about innovation. Open Innovation assumes that both internal as well as external ideas are utilized to create value and internal ideas can also be taken to market through external channels. Chesbrough addresses the importance of business models in augmenting the innovative capability (create and capture value that is created in the open R&D system) that can lead to competitive advantage. In his model he identifies the firm, as a combiner of ideas, knowledge and technology and explicitly points out that managers must actively manage knowledge flows within the company. Furthermore, Chesbrough emphasizes the role of intellectual property (IP) management and the rise of intermediaries in the innovation market.

In the latest years, Open Innovation has become a topic of great interest to academics and practitioners alike and various approaches and practices have been discussed in an ever growing body of literature (Chesbrough, 2003b,

Chesbrough, 2006, Chesbrough, 2003a, Enkel et al., 2009, Gassmann, 2006, Huston, 2006, von Hippel, 1988).

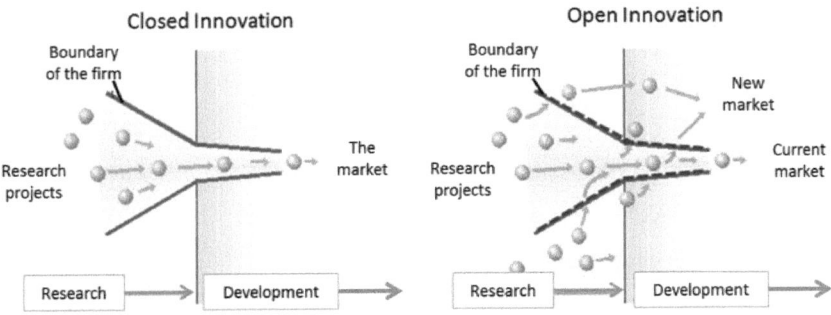

Figure 2 Contrasting principles of Closed and Open Innovation (adopted from Chesbrough 2006).

Figure 2 is a simplified representation of the Closed and Open Innovation concept. In Closed Innovation, a company generates, develops and commercializes its own ideas and technologies. Projects can only enter through one way, at the beginning, and exit in one way, by going into the market. This philosophy of self-reliance dominated the R&D operations of many leading industrial corporations for most of the 20th century.

In the Open Innovation model, a company commercializes both its own ideas as well as innovations from other firms and seeks ways to bring its in-house ideas to market by deploying pathways outside its current businesses. The boundary between the company and its surrounding environment is porous (represented in Figure 2 by dashed lines), enabling innovations to move more easily between the two. Here projects can be launched from either internal or external sources and new technologies can enter into the innovation process at any time. Additionally, projects can enter the market through many ways, such as e.g. through outsourcing or spin-off venture company or through the company's own marketing and sales channels.

1.2. Innovation-related online communities

Within the concept of Open Innovation the number of input channels has been increased. Thus, different methods, approaches and tools for an effective exchange of knowledge within and outside of the company have emerged over the years. These have been utilized successfully by many companies from different industries. Methods and approaches such as e.g. brainstorming, the lead-user approach (von Hippel, 1988, von Hippel, 2006) and participatory ergonomics (Kaulio, 1998) have been identified and largely discussed in academic literature. Additionally, and thanks to the recent developments in information and communication technologies (ICTs) companies have been given new possibilities to make use of the external ubiquitous and easily accessible online information – thus making Open Innovation easier to conduct.

In recent years a number of different innovation-related virtual communities have emerged and some are maintained by Open Innovation intermediaries also called virtual knowledge brokers (Verona et al., 2006) (Figure 3). Open Innovation intermediaries are platforms that foster virtual communities which can be composed of different groups of individuals who are interested in contributing and solving market relevant challenges. The community members can, for example, be scientific specialists, retired specialists or even ordinary individuals with different backgrounds. Typically, Open Innovation intermediaries operate a virtual community, manage the information flow between companies and the community and provide appropriate tools and advice about the utilization of the Open Innovation approach. Literature has cited specialized Open Innovation intermediaries, such as Innocentive or Ninesigma as examples of how ICTs have opened up novel possibilities for companies to enrich and, to some extent, modify their conventional innovation processes (Lakhani and Boudreau, 2009; Pisanno and Verganti, 2008).

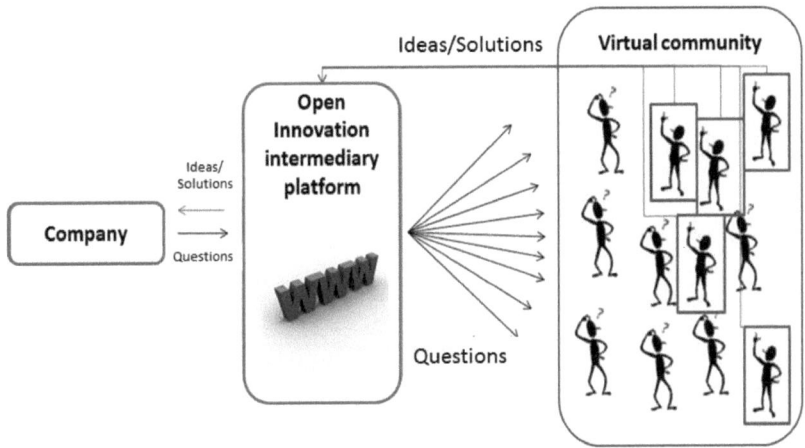

Figure 3 Intermediary-mediated Open Innovation model.

Other innovation-related communities are company-hosted. These are either public in the form of e.g. an online ideas platform such as IdeaStorm of the company Dell or Tschibo's Tschibo ideas. The focus of these platforms is to actively collect knowledge from different stakeholders such as e.g. customers, designers or suppliers. Company-hosted Open Innovation platforms can also be designed to collect internal knowledge from employees such as e.g. Swarovski's iflash idea management or Bombardier Aerospace, internal Open Innovation community (Figure 4).

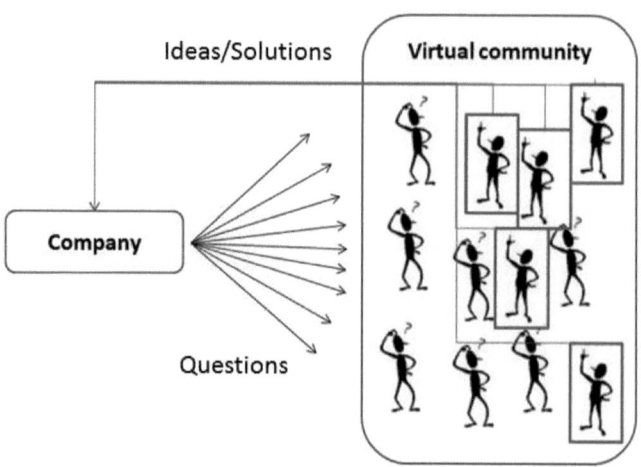

Figure 4 Company-hosted internal Open Innovation model.

Innovation-related virtual communities have drawn much attention in the field of innovation management and are increasingly being utilized by companies from different industries as a tool to efficiently source knowledge from diverse groups of individuals to nourish internal innovations. One important advantage related to the utilization of virtual communities is the possibility of companies to reach a large mass of individuals easily and at a relatively low cost.

1.3. Crowdsourcing

In 2004 James Sourowiecki argued in his book The wisdom of crowds: why the many are smarter than the few and how collective wisdom shapes business, economies, societies and nations (Surowiecki, 2004) that information extracted from groups, results in decisions that are often better than if they had been made by any single member of the group. Supported amongst others by these deliberations and the facilitated access to a large number of people around the globe via the Internet, the idea of Crowdsourcing, a recent Internet enabled Open Innovation approach was born. The term Crowdsourcing, first introduced by Jeff Howe (Howe, 2006) in the Wired Magazine, is increasingly used to describe a trend that has become one of the most talked about methods of Open Innovation. In its broad definition Crowdsourcing is described as outsourcing tasks traditionally performed by an employee or a contractor to a large group of people or a community (crowd) through an open call online. The contribution of external knowledge is hence made possible by advanced ICTs such as the Internet or mobile phones (Ebner et al., 2009, Fichter, 2009). In most cases, participants have no guaranteed reward. Recently, several papers have described successful practices of Crowdsourcing in various fields such as in design, R&D or marketing (Ebner et al., 2009, Piller and Walcher, 2006, Kirschbaum, 2005). The classic example of Crowdsourcing was developed in 2001 in the private sector by the pharmaceutical company Eli Lilly. Initially Innocentive was an initiative that was launched when the drug company faced a problem in designing a new product. Despite its large internal R&D department, the company had trouble solving a specific problem for developing a new product. A novel matchmaking system was developed to link company external experts to unsolved internal R&D problems. A monetary reward was offered to anyone who could solve the problem. Scientists from all over the world participated and competed for the prize. Finally, the winner got the prize and the company received a solution at a comparatively inexpensive price (Steve, 2006, Allio, 2004). This spawned a new company, InnoCentive, which today offers this approach to other companies. Nowadays, Crowdsourcing is often used as a standard approach for idea generation in the early innovation phase by companies from different industries (Bonabeau, 2009; Ebner et al., 2009). Some examples are IBM's 'Innovation jam', Procter & Gamble's 'connect+develop', Starbucks' 'My Starbucks idea', Lego's 'Mindstorms' and 'Design by me', Burdas 'BurdaStyle' and Fiats 'Fiat Mio'.

1.4. Open Innovation in the context of adoption of novel technologies

According to the innovation diffusion theory, first described by Everett M. Rogers (Rogers, 1962, Rogers, 2003) the willingness of individuals to adapt innovations vary. He identified five categories with members of each category typically possessing certain distinguishing characteristics, as illustrated below. In general individuals that first adopt an innovation require a shorter adoption period (adoption process) than late adopters.

- Innovators: venturesome, educated, multiple information sources.
- Early adopters: social leaders, popular, educated.
- Early majority: deliberate, many informal social contacts.
- Late majority: sceptical, traditional, lower socioeconomic status.
- Laggards: neighbours and friends are main information source, fear of debt.

Furthermore, Rogers has shown that five independent attributes have an impact on the rate of adoption of innovations:

- Relative advantage: the degree to which an innovation is perceived as being better than the idea it supersedes.
- Compatibility: an innovation is perceived as consistent with existing value, past experience and the needs of potential adopters.
- Complexity: an innovation is perceived as relatively difficult to understand and use.
- Trialability: an innovation may be experimented with on a limited basis.
- Observability: the results of an innovation are visible to others.

The first four factors are being described as generally positively correlated with the rate of adoption, while complexity is generally negatively correlated with the rate of adoption.

Building on this theory we assume that understanding the perceptions of users towards a particular technology or innovation early on in the innovation process can aid in creating innovations that are better fitting to the needs of the users. This may potentially improve the subsequent adoption process.

Due to the fact that a great number of innovative products and services are directly initiated by customers or are derived from specific customer needs or collected customer information (Lettl, 2004), it is crucial to understand these needs as well as how to integrate customer knowledge at an early stage of the innovation process. Once understood, the entire value chain of the innovation can be better directed towards accurate market needs. Discussions regarding integration of customer knowledge into the innovation process were initiated in the early 1980's and gained new recognition in the Open Innovation paradigm (Chesbrough, 2003a). Researchers and practitioners alike recommend companies to align their key product development activities with the needs of actual and potential customers in order to reduce failure risk, target resource spending and accelerate market adoption (Jaworski and Kohli, 1993, Bacon et al., 1994, Atuahene-Gima, 2005, Murphy and Kumar, 1997). In the past years companies have been increasingly utilizing the innovation resources, capabilities and knowledge of customers as well as other stakeholders such as e.g. suppliers to feed the innovation process in an early phase (Hagedoorn and Duysters, 2002, Muller and Välikangas, 2002, Rigby, 2002, Chesbrough, 2003a). The Open Innovation paradigm states that the innovation potential of stakeholders outside the company must be captured. This has become increasingly important for both practice and theory in the past years.

2. Aim of Research and Research Questions

The early phase of an innovation process, the so called upfront or fuzzy front-end of new product development, has been defined as the stages from idea generation to the stage where a decision for further development is taken (Murphy, 1997, Cooper, 1988). In this phase an organization formulates a product concept and determines whether or not to invest further resources to develop the idea (Moenaert et al., 1995). Literature has identified the early phases of the new product development to contribute directly to success in product innovation (Cooper, 1988, Dwyer, 1991, Verworn, 2009, McGuinness and Conway, 1989). Thus competency in managing the different stages of the fuzzy front-end is crucial in creating new product success.

In recent literature it has been shown that the Open Innovation approach Crowdsourcing is often applied in the early stage of the innovation process and particularly for idea generation (examples see 1.2.2.). Since idea generation has been shown to be a major contributor to a successful product innovation, it is important to understand the nature and the outcome of the process in the context of Open Innovation. Although researchers have investigated and described many successful Crowdsourcing cases there are still limited empirical examinations of the underlying Crowdsourcing process in general as well as factors affecting the outcome.

The aim of this research is to investigate the following three points as well as provide relate recommendations useful for practice:

a) Gaining in-depth insights and improve the understanding of the intermediary-mediated Crowdsourcing process.

b) Investigate factors affecting the motivation of community members to participate and collaborate in intermediary and company-hosted innovation-related virtual communities.

The research questions were thus defined as follows:

1. How do companies plan, setup and conduct intermediary-mediated Crowdsourcing processes for idea generation?

2. Which factors affect the motivation of community members to participate and collaborate in intermediary and company-hosted innovation-related virtual communities?

3. Research Methodology

The choice and combination of research methodologies was determined by the character of the research questions and research objectives.

3.1. The intermediary-mediated Crowdsourcing process

Intermediary mediated Crowdsourcing projects can be seen as continuous processes that typically require longitudinal observations (Pettigrew, 1990), prompting a case study design. Hence, for the in-depth investigation of the intermediary mediated Crowdsourcing process and in order to obtain insight into the process a thorough literature research was performed and an explorative multi-case study research design was applied to extract longitudinal data (Eisenhardt, 1989, Yin, 2003, Stake, 1995). Furthermore, qualitative as well as a quantitative data analysis were performed to achieve findings and results. It has recently been argued by Shah and Corley (2006) that combined analysis offer valuable insights. The following is a detailed methodology description of paper nr. 6.

3.1.1. Case study and Crowdsourcing intermediary selection

Data was collected from 12 individual Crowdsourcing projects performed by nine Swiss companies from four different industries, namely the insurance industry, the banking industry, the energy industry and the tourism industry (Table 1).

Company name	Industry	Name of project	Weeks online	# of ideas
Helsana	Healthcare	Sales of health insurance online	8	212
Helsana	Healthcare	Creation of an online campaign	8	165
KPT	Healthcare	New service: the online health platform	6	291
PostFinance	Banking	Creative ways to approach customers	8	248
PostFinance	Banking	Attractive online services for customers	8	269
KWRO	Tourism	Raising awareness about accident risks in ski regions	7	339
SBB mobiliar	Tourism	Customer friendly large train stations	7	490
Graubünden	Tourism	Community website Graubünden	8	365
EWB	Energy	Innovative energy provider	6	315
EWB	Energy	Individually mobile: energy from the power socket	9	428
Youtility	Energy	Gas products for households and small businesses	6	196
Bühler	Energy	Business model for energy consulting	10	177

Table 1 Detailed list of the Crowdsourcing projects conducted during this research.

There were three main reasons for selecting these cases: first, the Crowdsourcing projects were performed by companies from different industries. This allowed us to control and detect environmental variations. Second, we chose to study multiple cases within each industry in order to allow the replication of the findings within the industry group. Third, given the research focus to understand the underlying Crowdsourcing process, we searched for successfully performed Crowdsourcing projects. The criteria for a successful Crowdsourcing project are based on positive answers of the following questions taken from the last round of interviews:

1. Are you generally satisfied with the executed Crowdsourcing project?
2. After having gathered experiences with this intermediary mediated Crowdsourcing project, would you/your company utilize Crowdsourcing as an approach for idea generation in the future?
3. Will you utilize the results of the performed Crowdsourcing project to integrate in e.g., business plans, in product/service/process development or improvements?

The Crowdsourcing projects were executed on the online platform of the Swiss open innovation intermediary Atizo. Atizo was estimated to be an appropriate platform to investigate the Crowdsourcing process as it was an established Crowdsourcing intermediary supporting the idea generation process of various companies and had an online 'innovator' community consisting of on average 4'500 heterogeneous members with different backgrounds during 2009.

3.1.2. Data sources

This study relies on data collected during three rounds of semi-structured interviews conducted with two company participants from each of the 12 Crowdsourcing projects as well as interviews on a weekly basis with Atizo representatives throughout the entire research project duration (the entire year 2009). The interviews were conducted at the following project phases:

1st interview round: shortly before project initiation.

2nd interview round: two weeks after the online publication of the Crowdsourcing question.

3rd interview round: approximately one month after project termination.

The participants were given the opportunities to share their experiences and thoughts, state opinions and narrate stories. In total, 72 interviews were conducted and lasted on average 60 min. The interview guidelines for all three interview rounds had some similarities in order to capture possible change. The first interview round included, amongst others, questions regarding the company and its positioning in the industry, its innovation culture, its conventional innovation processes, perceived utility and compatibility of the Crowdsourcing project, motivation, perceived potential/risks and drivers/inhibitors in connection with the Crowdsourcing project and the online intermediary Crowdsourcing platform. The second interview round included questions regarding satisfaction with the ongoing Crowdsourcing project, any occurring special issues, expectation towards the Crowdsourcing project and the results, perceived or experienced success/risk factors and drivers/inhibitors. The third interview round included questions revealing the different opinions towards the Crowdsourcing project, lessons learned and future intentions with the achieved results. The Crowdsourcing process phases were identified through parallel comparison of the three interview rounds, which were identical for all 12 Crowdsourcing projects. For each answer points of similarities and differences between the 12 Crowdsourcing projects were identified and a primary structure of the Crowdsourcing process and its different phases were thereby extracted. This scaffold was gradually further developed until all essential details were included and documented leading to the emergence of the detailed intermediary mediated Crowdsourcing process.

3.1.3. Project details

The questions were posted, and made visible for the innovator community, on Atizo's online platform between April 9, 2009 and September 4, 2009. The questions were online for a total duration of six to ten weeks (Table 1). The community was restricted by Atizo to submit contributions containing a maximum of 150 words and one image. However, rating and commenting tools were available to community members and companies during the idea generation phase. Table 1 illustrates that different amounts of ideas were submitted to each Crowdsourcing project and on average more than 260 ideas were generated within six to ten weeks.

3.2. Motivation factors of community members in Crowdsourcing

In order to improve the understanding of factors affecting community members' motivation to participate and contribute in two different types of innovation-related communities, i.e. company-hosted internal innovation community and intermediary innovation community, we applied an empirical multi-case study research design (Eisenhardt, 1989, Stake, 1995). The findings are based on data collected by means of an e-survey which was sent to the two communities and subsequently analyzed quantitatively. The following is a detailed methodology description of paper nr. 5.

3.2.1. Case studies

Data sets were collected from the internal innovation community of PostFinance and the intermediary innovation community of Atizo. PostFinance is a Swiss bank and an employer of roughly 3'000 people. In 2010, PostFinance initiated the internal innovation community as a pilot project to test the Crowdsourcing approach for internal idea generation. Atizo is a prominent Swiss Open Innovation intermediary which operates a community consisting of approximately 8'000 members (2010) with heterogeneous interests and background.

3.2.2. Data sources and project details

Following a thorough literature research and an internal deliberation, an e-survey was designed to include 39 motivation factors and the questions were sent to members of the two studied innovation communities. All of the items in the e-survey were presented as statements to which contributors were asked to state their personal perceived importance on a five-point Likert scale of 1 to 5 (1= "Unimportant", 2= "Partially unimportant", 3. "Neutral", 4. "Important", 5. "Very important"). A brief description of our study and the link to the e-survey was sent to 121 community members and employees of PostFinance. These all had been chosen internally from different departments to participate in the pilot project and each had at least submitted one idea during a previous idea generation project. Simultaneously, a brief description of our study and the link to the e-survey was integrated in Atizos monthly community newsletter and additionally posted on Atizos Facebook, Twitter, and Blog page. The two independent e-surveys were performed in August 2010 and returned within three or two weeks, respectively. 69 PostFinance employees and 48 Atizo community members completed the e-survey. The e-surveys were performed using the online tool Unipark and results were analyzed with PASW (SPSS) statistics software.

3.3. Application of Open Innovation approaches

Various publications resulting from this research applied Open Innovation approaches such as Crowdsourcing stakeholder integration (i.e. Customers, business partners) and delivered insight about how effectively Open Innovation can be applied in practice (Table 3). Findings of these publications were a result of thorough literature research and an empirical case study research methodology based on face-to-face interviews, teleconferences and e-surveys. Depending on the nature of the data, qualitative and quantitative analysis were performed.

4. Key findings

This research project has resulted in several important findings related to the area of Open Innovation and in particular regarding the latest Open Innovation approach: Internet enabled Crowdsourcing. Furthermore, manager implications have been suggested and discussed on the basis of the results as well as observations throughout the multiple projects.

4.1. The Crowdsourcing process

The intermediary-mediated Crowdsourcing process was thoroughly investigated, defined and the overall understanding of how it is applied for idea generation in the early innovation process was depicted. The following five phases of the intermediary-mediated Crowdsourcing process were identified to be important and are illustrated in Figure 5.

    1) the deliberation phase
    2) the preparation phase
    3) the execution phase

4) the assessment phase
5) the post-processing phase

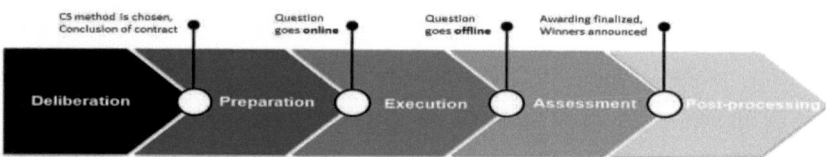

Figure 5 Five important phases of the intermediary-meditated Crowdsourcing process.

Additionally, the most important tasks within each phase were identified and elaborated on. Figure 6 is a simplified overview of the overall results of this research. It illustrates the identified five phases of the intermediary-mediated Crowdsourcing process and their important tasks.

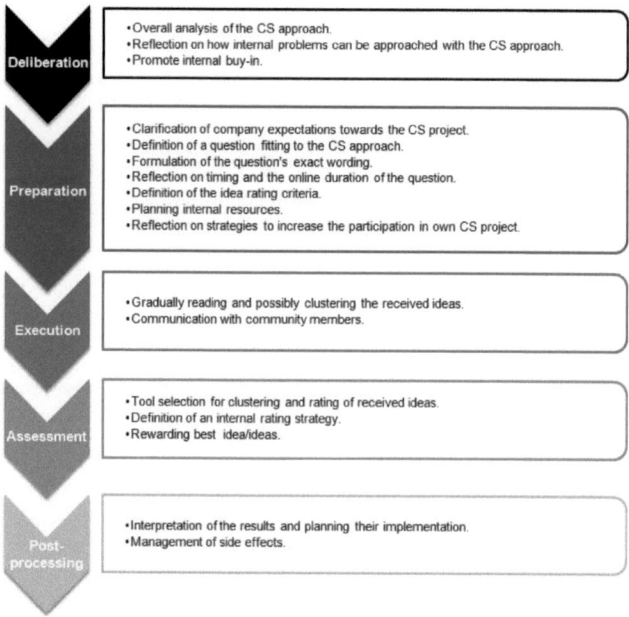

Figure 6: Five phases of the intermediary-mediated Crowdsourcing process and their important tasks.

We found the tasks in the first two phases (deliberation and preparation) to be particularly decisive for the success of a Crowdsourcing project due to the virtual and Open Innovation context. The decisions made here are definitive and cannot be corrected in later phases unlike, e.g., during a traditional idea generation workshop where a closed group of people meet physically. Additionally, we emphasize the importance of the activities after idea evaluation (post-processing). Since the results are generated externally, an additional effort for interpretation and implementation into the company's context is essential.

4.2. Motivation factors important for members' participation and contribution in innovation-related online communities.

The two innovation communities investigated in this study, i.e. the community of the innovation intermediary Atizo and the internal innovation community of the Swiss bank PostFinance, showed similarities as well as differences in how important they perceive the investigated 39 motivational items to be for their participation and contribution. In order to simplify the interpretation of the findings, the 39 motivational items were aggregated and the following six categories were defined: 1) Social aspect, 2) Competition, 3) Learning, 4) Sense of efficiency, 5) Rewards and 6) Platform features (Figure 7).

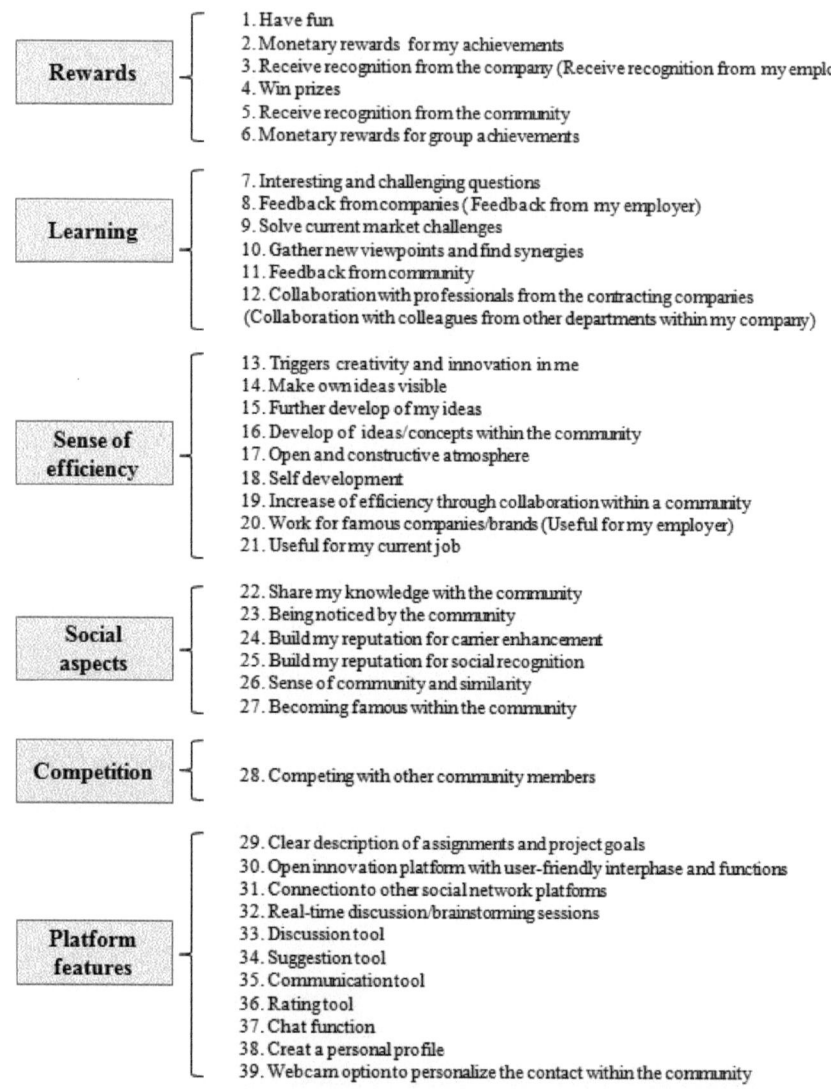

Figure 7 In this study investigated motivation factors categorized into six categories. Formulations of the items for the internal innovation community that differ from the intermediary community are in brackets.

To support detection of potential trends and to facilitate data interpretation, a simple depiction of the achieved data was performed aiming to illustrate the ranking of the six categories for the two innovation communities (Table 1). The rankings are based on the average of the mean values of the items within each category where the items were given equal weight.

Category ranking	Intermediary community (Mean value)	Internal community (Mean value)
1	Rewards (3.97)	Learning (3.88)
2	Learning (3.91)	Sense of efficiency (3.84)
3	Sense of efficiency (3.69)	Platform features (3.09)
4	Platform features (3.21)	Social aspects (3.05)
5	Social aspects (3.09)	Rewards (2.88)
6	Competition (2.71)	Competition (2.41)

Table 2 Category ranking intermediary vs. internal innovation community.

Findings have shown that there is a significant difference between the perceived importance of Rewards for participation and contribution between the intermediary innovation community and the company-hosted internal innovation community.

In coherence with the findings of a previous paper (Antikainen and Väätäjä, 2010) the findings indicate that intermediary community members who contribute on a voluntarily base find a combination of monetary and non-monetary rewards to be an important trade-offs for their individual contribution. Additionally, 'Have fun' was found to be the top motivator for these individuals. Members of the company-hosted internal community, however, did not weigh any items belonging to the category 'Rewards' as important for their motivation to participate and contribute within the innovation community.

In general, the importance of the perceived learning aspects was rather high for both innovation communities. Top motivators were found in the category

'Learning' and suggest that the intermediary community finds it important to be informed about and work on actual business challenges. Members of the internal community on the other hand showed to attach great importance to the educational effect. They find it important that the community aids to broaden their own horizon and can be used to identify colleagues in possession of similar ideas and thoughts. They additionally found the possible emergence of internal collaborations important.

Surprisingly, many items which appeared on the lowest end of the items rankings of the two innovation communities were identical. These items belong to the categories 'Platform features', 'Competition' and 'Social aspects' and were the following: 'Webcam option', 'Competition with other community members', 'Chat function', 'Connection to other social networking platforms', 'Becoming famous within the community', 'Create a personal profile', 'Real-time discussions/brainstorming sessions'.

Interestingly, the competition factor showed not to be an important motivation to participate and contribute in either of the two Swiss innovation communities.

5. Implications for Further Research

This research makes several important contributions to current literature.

First, we have identified and described the Crowdsourcing process to be composed of five phases and emphasized important tasks within each phase, which should to be considered when engaging in a Crowdsourcing project. Our research generally adds to the idea generation and online idea competition literature and more precisely to the limited empirical examinations about intermediary-mediated Crowdsourcing by providing insight into how companies engage in these processes and which challenges they face during the different phases. Because an idea by itself is far from being a profitable product or a service, further research should focus on the implementation of the ideas or overall results achieved through Crowdsourcing projects. This research can provide valuable insight about e.g. the success rate of the Crowdsourcing projects in different companies. In this context, interesting insights might be won on how and in which form the achieved results can be incorporated into internal processes within the companies. Moreover, it is valuable to understand which factors influence the quality of the virtually generated ideas and its results.

Second, our research has increased the understanding of motivation factors affecting the participation and contribution of members in innovation related communities. It highlights the similarities and differences in perceived importance of different motivation factors between two different innovation communities, i.e. a Swiss innovation intermediary community and an internal innovation community of a Swiss bank. Understanding factors affecting contribution and active involvement in innovation communities is of significance to increase project success.

While the findings of this part of the research are based on e-surveys conducted with existing community members, it is important to know the motivations of non-community members as well. Furthermore, the link between motivation and quality of the submissions and important factors motivating 'appropriate' contributors is likely to be of interest to innovation researchers and managers.

This research has focused largely on Crowdsourcing for idea generation. Further research should as well investigate the application of Crowdsourcing in different stages of the value chain.

6. Articles and summaries

The research projects presented in this doctoral dissertation has resulted in 10 articles which have been published in important international scientific and practitioner journals. The articles answer research questions and provide recommendations to theory as well as to practice. Table 3 illustrates a list of all published articles and the print version of the 3 articles most relevant in the context of this book can be found in the Appendix (section 8).

Article No.	Title of article	Authors	Journal/ Book	Date of publication	Review
1	Factors affecting community members' motivation to participate and contribute in Crowdsourcing projects	L. Muhdi, R. Boutellier	The international Journal of Innovation Management (IJIM)	Published 2011	Double blinded peer review
2	Crowdsourcing: Unveiling motivation factors affecting participation and contribution in Swiss innovation communities	L. Muhdi, R. Boutellier	The proceedings of the 3rd ISPIM Innovation Symposium "Managing the art of innovation: turning concepts to reality", Quebec, Canada, December 12-15th, 2010. ISBN 978-952-265-004-7.	Published 2010	Double blinded peer review
3	The Crowdsourcing process: an intermediary mediated idea generation approach in the early phase of innovation	L. Muhdi, M. Daiber, S. Fiesike, R. Boutellier	The international Journal of Entrepreneurship and Innovation Management (IJEIM)	Published 2011	Double blinded peer review
4	Der Crowdsourcing-Prozess	O. Gassmann, M. Daiber, L. Muhdi	Book: "Crowdsourcing - Innovationsmanagement mit Schwarmintelligenz". München : Hanser, 2010, S. 21-44. ISBN 3-446-42334-6.	Published 2010	Editor's review

5	Crowdsourcing: an alternative idea generation approach in the early innovation process	L. Muhdi, M. Daiber, S. Fiesike, R. Boutellier	The proceedings of the XXI ISPIM Conference on "The Dynamics of Innovation", Bilbao, Spain, June 6-9, 2010. ISBN 978-952-214-926.	Published 2010	Double blinded peer review
6	Study for Small-Space Retailer: Crowdsourcing for "Kiosk of the Future"	E. D. Spiegler, L. Muhdi	The proceedings of the 17th Americas Conference on Information Systems (AMCIS)	Published 2011	Double blinded peer review
7	Discovering the success factors of Buddysourcing: A case of online job recruitment	F. Magagna L. Muhdi, J. Sutanto	The proceedings of the 3rd ISPIM Innovation Symposium "Managing the art of innovation: turning concepts to reality", Quebec, Canada, December 12-15, 2010. ISBN 978-952-265-004-7.	Published 2010	Double blinded peer review
8	Diffusion of potential health-related e-service an analysis of Swiss health insurance customer perspectives	L. Muhdi, R. Boutellier	Journal of Management & Marketing in Healthcare (JMMH)	Published 2010	Double blinded peer review
9	Mobile contactless payment and Mobile Ticketing – a Swiss status report (EN/DE)	L. Muhdi, M. Raus, R. Boutellier	KPMG publications	Published 2010	Editor's review
10	Wie viel Innovation erträgt die Medizin?	R. Boutellier, L. Muhdi	SAR: Die schweizerische Arzt & Spital-Revue	Published 2009	Editor's review

Table 3 Detailed list of all articles produced during this research.

6.1. The Crowdsourcing process: an intermediary mediated idea generation approach in the early phase of innovation.

L. Muhdi, M. Daiber, S. Friesike, R. Boutellier (2011)

International Journal of. Entrepreneurship and Innovation Management, Vol. 14, No. 4, 201. Copyright @ 2011, Inderscience publishers.

Internet-based Crowdsourcing is nowadays adopted by various companies in different industries. Even though many success stories have been described, little is known about the Crowdsourcing process for idea generation in the early innovation process. An explorative and qualitative multi-case study research methodology was applied to extract the longitudinal data that was analyzed in this research. Findings of this research are based on twelve Crowdsourcing projects executed by nine Swiss companies on the Swiss intermediary Crowdsourcing platform Atizo.

Findings: This research has delivered the following insights: First, the intermediary mediated Crowdsourcing process was found to be composed of the following five successional phases: 1. The deliberation phase, 2. The preparation phase, 3. The execution phase, 4. The assessment phase and 5. The post-processing phase. Second, important tasks within each phase which ought to be considered when engaging in a Crowdsourcing project were described and recommendations given to increase project success and company satisfaction. Third, analogies between Herbert A. Simons' decision making model and the Crowdsourcing process were confirmed and the effect of the virtual and Open Innovation nature of the Crowdsourcing approach on the decision making processes in companies was discussed.

Conclusion: This research adds generally to the idea generation and online idea competition literature and more precisely to the limited empirical examinations about intermediary mediated Crowdsourcing. It provides insight into how companies engage in these processes and which challenges they face during the different phases. Furthermore recommendations are made to anticipate these challenges. Business professionals can utilize the insights of this paper to improve their understanding of the process underlying intermediary enabled virtual Crowdsourcing. In-depth understanding of the different phases and the associated tasks, the advantages and the limitations of the Crowdsourcing process can improve its application for idea generation and decision making support within the company. The findings can assist optimizing investigation how to implement Crowdsourcing in early innovation processes.

6.2. Crowdsourcing for "Kiosk of the Future" – A Retail Store Case Study

E. Dubach, , L. Muhdi, D. Stöcklin, F. Michahelles (2011)

Americas Conference on Information Systems (AMCIS) 2011 Proceedings - All Submissions. Paper 324. Copyright @ 2011, Publisher: Association for Information Systems (AIS).

This article reports on a case study which describes how Valora Retail, the company that operates the majority of Kiosks in Switzerland, successfully completed a intermediary mediated Crowdsourcing project as well as the results they achieved using this open innovation approach to generate ideas for the internal project named the "Kiosk of the Future".

Findings: Out of the 626 ideas virtually submitted by the Atizo community, 2/3 were considered irrelevant to Valora Retail and were not processed further. From the remaining 204 ideas (33%) 140 ideas (22%) were judged to be relevant for Valora Retail, but not relevant for the project "Kiosk of the Future". Therefore, only 64 ideas were evaluated to be relevant for the "Kiosk of the Future" project. The best 19 ideas were given rewards and were considered for further internal analysis and development. Five of the top 19 ideas from the Crowdsourcing process were assessed to be impossible to implement in a live Kiosk setting due to technological, logistical or business constraints and were put aside as source of inspiration or future options to be tested in a lab setting. The remaining 14 ideas were submitted to an "idea jury" made up of stakeholders from different departments of Valora Retail (Strategic Marketing, Corporate Communications, Kiosk Management, and Conception & Construction Management).

Conclusion: This case study clearly demonstrated a successful application of Crowdsourcing for idea generation and as feed for the early innovation process. It was reported that the achieved outcome of this project would unlikely have originated from the company itself due to high internal barriers. The insights gained by Valora Retail during the execution of the Crowdsourcing project helped the company to clearly distinguish between activities for the idea generation and those for the idea implementation and plan accordingly. The final low number of ideas that were chosen and approved for implementation (4 of total 626 submitted ideas) was rather surprising to the Crowdsourcing project leads. The experiences gathered throughout the project will in the future aid Valora Retail to better plan and organize resources at right moments for future Crowdsourcing projects.

6.3. Motivational factors affecting participation and contribution of members in two different Swiss innovation communities

L. Muhdi and R. Boutellier (2011)

International Journal of Innovation Management, Vol. 15, No. 3 (June 2011) pp. 543–562. Publisher: Copyright @ 2011, World Scientific Journals.

Various virtual innovation-related communities have emerged in recent years. These are increasingly being utilized by companies from different industries as a tool to efficiently source knowledge from diverse groups of individuals and to nourish internal innovations. Based on a quantitative case study research methodology this study investigated the impact that 39 motivation factors have on the participation and contribution of members of two different innovation communities, i.e. an online Swiss innovation intermediary community (n=48) and the off-line internal innovation community of a Swiss bank (n=69). The intermediary community is composed of individuals with different personal and professional backgrounds which voluntarily register as innovators with the Crowdsourcing intermediary company. The internal innovation community however is composed of company employees only.

Findings: Results showed similarities and differences between the two communities. For example, item such as 'Webcam option', 'Chat function', 'Connection with other social network platforms', were identified as low motivators in both communities whereas reward related items, monetary and non-monetary, showed to be top motivators for the intermediary community only.

Conclusion: Understanding factors affecting contribution and active involvement in innovation communities is of significance to increase project success. In that context, this study makes several important contributions to current literature. First, the findings increase the understanding of motivation factors affecting the participation and contribution of members in innovation related communities. Second, the results highlight similarities and differences in perceived importance of different motivation factors between two different innovation communities, i.e. a Swiss innovation intermediary community and an internal innovation community of a Swiss bank. Third, and based on the knowledge gained, suggestions for measurements are formulated to increase participation and contribution efficiency in intermediary and internal innovation communities.

7. References

ACHILLADELIS, B. & ANTONAKIS, N. (2001) The dynamics of technological innovation: the case of the pharmaceutical industry. Research Policy, 30, 535-588.

ALLIO, R., J. (2004) CEO interview: The InnoCentive model of open innovation. Strategy & Leadership, 32, 4-9.

ANTIKAINEN, M. & VÄÄTÄJÄ, H. (2010) Rewarding in open innovation communities - how to motivate members. International Journal of Entrepreneurship and Innovation Management, 11, 440-456.

ATUAHENE-GIMA, K. (2005) Resolving the capability rigidity paradox in new product innovation. Journal of marketing, 69, 61.

BACON, G., BECKMAN, S., MOWERY, D. & WILSON, E. (1994) Managing product definition in high-technology industries: a pilot study. California management review, 36, 32.

BOER, H. & DURING, W. E. (2001) Innovation, what innovation? A comparison between product, process and organizational innovation. International Journal of Technology Management, 22, 83-107.

BROWN, S. L. & EISENHARDT, K. M. (1995) PRODUCT DEVELOPMENT - PAST RESEARCH, PRESENT FINDINGS, AND FUTURE-DIRECTIONS. Academy of Management Review, 20, 343-378.

CHESBROUGH, H., VANHAVERBEKE, W. & WEST, J. (2006) Open Innovation: Researching a New Paradigm, New York, Oxford Universty Press.

CHESBROUGH, H. W. (2003a) The era of Open Innovation. Sloan Management Review, 44, 35-41.

CHESBROUGH, H. W. (2003b) Open innovation the new imperative for creating and profiting from technology, Boston, MA, Harvard Business School Press.

CHESBROUGH, H. W. (2006) Open innovation researching a new paradigm, Oxford, Oxford University Press.

COHEN, W. M. & LEVINTHAL, D. A. (1990) Absorptive Capacity: A New Perspective on Learning and Innovation. Administrative Science Quarterly, 35, 128-152.

COOPER, R. G. (1988) Predevelopment activities determine new product success. Industrial Marketing Management, 17, 237-247.

COOPER, R. G. (2000) WINNING WITH NEW PRODUCTS: DOING IT RIGHT. Ivey Business Journal, 64, 54.

DE BRENTANI, U. (2001) Innovative versus incremental new business services: Different keys for achieving success. Journal of Product Innovation Management, 18, 169-187.

DOMBROWSKI, C., KIM, J. Y., DESOUZA, K. C., BRAGANZA, A., PAPAGARI, S., BALOH, P. & JHA, S. (2007) Elements of innovative cultures. Knowledge and Process Management, 14, 190-202.

DRUCKER, P. F. (1986) The frontiers of management where tomorrow's decisions are being shaped today, New York, Truman Talley Books.

DWYER, L., AND MELLOR, R. (1991) Organizational environment, new product process activities, and project outcomes. Journal of Product Innovation Management, 8, 39-48.

EBNER, W., LEIMEISTER, J. M. & KRCMAR, H. (2009) Community engineering for innovations: the ideas competition as a method to nurture a virtual community for innovations. R&D Management, 39, 342-356.

EISENHARDT, K. M. (1989) Building Theories from Case Study Research. Academy of Management Review. Academy of Management.

ENKEL, E., GASSMANN, O. & CHESBROUGH, H. (2009) Open R&D and open innovation; exploring the phenomenon. R&D Management, 39, 311 - 316.

FICHTER, K. (2009) Innovation communities; the role of networks in Open Innovation. R&D Management, 39, 357-371.

FRIEDEL, R. (Ed.) (2007) A culture of Improvement: Technology and the Western Millenium, MIT press.

GASSMANN, O. (2006) Opening up the innovation process: towards an agenda. R&D Management, 36, 223-228.

HAGEDOORN, J. & DUYSTERS, G. (2002) External sources of innovative capabilities: the preferences for strategic alliances or mergers and acquisitions. Journal of Management Studies, 39, 167-188.

HAN, J. K., KIM, N. & SRIVASTAVA, R. K. (1998) Market orientation and organizational performance: Is innovation a missing link? Journal of Marketing, 62, 30-45.

HOWE, J. (2006) The Rise of Crowdsourcing. Wired Magazine.

HURLEY, R. F. (1998) Innovation, market orientation, and organizational learning: An integration and empirical examination. Journal of Marketing, 62, 42-54.

HUSTON, L., SAKKAB, N. (2006) Connect and develop: Inside Procter & Gamble's new model for innovation. Harvard business review 84, 58.

JAWORSKI, B., J. & KOHLI, A., K. (1993) Market orientation: antecedents and consequences. Journal of marketing, 57.

KAULIO, M. A. (1998) Customer, consumer and user involvement in product development: A framework and a review of selected methods. Total Quality Management, 9, 141-149.

KIRSCHBAUM, R. (2005) Open Innovation in Practice. Research-Technology Management, 48, 24-38.

LETTL, C. (2004) Die Rolle von Anwendern bei hochgradigen Innovationen eine explorative Fallstudienanalyse in der Medizintechnik. Wiesbaden, Deutscher Universitäts-Verlag.

MCGUINNESS, N. W. & CONWAY, H. A. (1989) Managing the search for new product concepts - a strategic approach. R & D Management, 19, 297-308.

MOENAERT, R. K., DEMEYER, A., SOUDER, W. E. & DESCHOOLMEESTER, D. (1995) R&D marketing communication during the fuzzy front-end. IEEE Transactions on Engineering Management, 42, 243-258.

MOTWANI, J., DANDRIDGE, T., JIANG, J. & SODERQUIST, K. (1999) Managing Innovation in French Small and Medium-Sized Enterprises. Journal of Small Business Management, 37, 106-114.

MULLER, A. & VÄLIKANGAS, L. (2002) Extending the boundary of corporate innovation. Strategy & Leadership, 30, 4-9.

MURPHY, S. A., AND KUMER, V. (1997) The front end of new product development: a Canadian survey. R&D Management, 27, 5-15.

MURPHY, S. A. & KUMAR, V. (1997) The front end of new product development: A Canadian survey. R & D Management, 27, 5-15.

NORTH, D. & SMALLBONE, D. (2000) The innovativeness and growth of rural SMEs during the 1990s. Regional Studies, 34, 145-157.

PILLER, F. T. & WALCHER, D. (2006) Toolkits for idea competitions: a novel method to integrate users in new product development. R&D Management.

RIGBY, D. K., AND ZOOK, C. (2002) Open-market innovation. Harvard Business Review, 80, 80-89.

ROGERS, E. M. (1962) Diffusion of innovations, New York, Free Press.

ROGERS, E. M. (2003) Diffusion of innovations, New York, Free Press.

SCHUMPETER (1927) The explanation of the business cycle. Economica, VII, 286-311.

SCHUMPETER, J. A. (1943) Capitalism, Socialism and Democracy, London, Allen and Unwin.

STAKE, R. E. (1995) The art of case study research, Thousand Oaks, California [etc.], Sage Publications.

STEVE, R. (2006) Who's ready to crowdsource? Advertising Age, 77, 35.

SUROWIECKI, J. (2004) The wisdom of crowds why the many are smarter than the few and how collective wisdom shapes business, economies, societies, and nations, London, Little.

THAMHAIN, H. J. (2003) Managing innovative R&D teams. R & D Management, 33, 297-311.

VERWORN, B. (2009) A structural equation model of the impact of the "fuzzy front end" on the success of new product development. Research Policy, 38, 1571-1581.

VON HIPPEL, E. (1988) The sources of innovation, New York [etc.], Oxford University Press.

VON HIPPEL, E. (2006) Democratizing innovation, Cambridge, Mass., MIT Press.

YIN, R. K. (2003) Case study research design and methods, Thousand Oaks, Sage Publications

8. Appendix

8.1. List of Interviews

Company ID	Interviewee	Position	Content	Location	Date
KOF ETHZ	Spyros Arvanitis	Head of Devision	Innovation Park Dübendorf	Zurich	Mar 2008
Kinderspital	Roger Lauener	Head of Department Immunology	Telemedicine	Zurich	Apr 08
ÖKK	Peter Werder	Head of communication	ICT in Healthcare	Landquart	Apr 08
Groupe Mutuel	Yves Seydoux	Head of Comunication	ICT in Healthcare	Berne	Apr 08
Concordia	Erich Krügel	Head of Marketing	ICT in Healthcare	Lucerne	Apr 08
RVK	Marcel Graber	Director	ICT in Healthcare	Lucerne	Apr 08
Atupri	Karl Luca Büeler	Head of Marketing	ICT in Healthcare	Berne	Apr 08
KPT	Ethienne Habegger	CEO	ICT in Healthcare	Berne	Apr 08
CSS	Marco Ippolito	Head of CRM & Internet	ICT in Healthcare	Lucerne	Apr 08
Precious Woods	Felix Howald	Chief Sustainability & Business Development Officer	Student Master Thesis	Zurich	Jun 08
Medi24	Roman Feierabend	Director IT Services	Student Master Thesis	Berne	Jul 08
Medgate	Andy Fischer	CEO	Telemedicine	Basel	Jul 08

Company	Name	Role	Topic	Location	Date
Atizo	Christian Hirsig	CEO	KTI-Open Innovation	Berne	2008-2010
Inch	Christian Häuselman	CEO	KTI-Open Innovation	Berne	2008-2010
Nestlé PTC	Florence Mathieu	Innovation Management	KTI-Open Innovation	Konolfingen	Mar 09
Nestlé PTC	Anthony Strong	Innovation Management	KTI-Open Innovation	Konolfingen	Mar 09
Open Systems	Martin Bosshardt	CEO	Student Master Thesis	Zurich	Apr 09
Julius Bär	Frank Flügel	Strategic Marketing	KTI-Open Innovation	Zurich	2009-2010
KPT	Reto Egloff	Head of Marketing and Destitution	KTI-Open Innovation	Berne	2009-2010
KPT	Tamara Berger	Head of online services	KTI-Open Innovation	Berne	2009-2010
PostFinance	Beat Steiner	Market Manager	KTI-Open Innovation	Berne	2009-2010
PostFinance	Cyril Schaad	Innovation Management	KTI-Open Innovation	Berne	2009-2010
PostFinance	Alexander Graf	Marketing Communication	KTI-Open Innovation	Berne	2009-2010
Helsana	Matthias Stöckli	Head of E&M Commerce	KTI-Open Innovation	Dübendorf	2009-2010
KPMG	Hans-Ulrich Pfyffer	Partner, Swiss Certificated Accounts	Mobile Technology	Zurich	2009-2010
Credit Suisse	Christoph Hugentobler	Assistant Vice President, Innovation Manager, Banking Products & support	KTI-Open Innovation	Zurich	Aug 09
SIX Multipay AG	Thomas Landis	Head of Innovation & Development	Mobile Technology	Zurich	Aug 09
Sunrise Communication	Kai-Uwe Seelig	Manager Multimedia Residential	Mobile Technology-	Zurich	Aug 09

		Customers	NFC Study		
PostFinance	Thierry Kneissler	Head of Business Development	Mobile Technology-NFC Study	Berne	Sep 09
PostFinance	Hannes Burkhalter	Consultant cooperations & Strategy	Mobile Technology-NFC Study	Berne	Sep 09
PostFinance	Roland Greber	Project Head mobile Payments	Mobile Technology-NFC Study	Berne	Sep 09
UBS	Cord-Constantin Bregulla	Head of Card Soulutions	Mobile Technology-NFC Study	Zurich	Sep 09
PostAuto Schweiz AG	Delphine Albrecht	Marketing & Strategy	Mobile Technology-NFC Study	Berne	Sep 09
Aduno Group	Peter Durrer	Project Manager New Services Management	Mobile Technology-NFC Study	Glattbrugg	Sep 09
Trüb	Stephan Breitenmoser	Sales Director Switzerland	Mobile Technology-NFC Study	Zurich	Sep 09
Raffeisen	Othmar Fritschi	Head of Product Management, Payment Products and Systems	Mobile Technology-NFC Study	St. Gallen	Sep 09
Ticketcorner	Martin Lüdicke	Director Product Management	Mobile Technology-NFC Study	Zurich	Sep 09
MasterCard Worldwide	Rolf Janssen	Head of Europe	Mobile Technology-NFC Study	Zurich	Sep 09
Selecta	Thomas Kurzen	Head of Development	Mobile Technology-NFC Study	Zug	Sep 09
Selecta	Markus Egger	Head of Group Technology Management	Mobile Technology-NFC Study	Zug	Sep 09
Coop	Laurent Bernasconi	Processes and Sales	Mobile Technology-NFC Study	Basel	Jul 05

Company	Name	Position	Topic	Location	Date
Credit Suisse	Alexander Verbeck	Product Management Debit & Cash Services	Mobile Technology-NFC Study	Dübendorf	Sep 09
Swisscard	Rolf Wyssling	Relationship Manager, Consumer Business	Mobile Technology-NFC Study	Horgen	Sep 09
Migros	Paul Beck	Head of IT	Mobile Technology-NFC Study	Zurich	Sep 09
Legic	Christoph Aschmoneit	Technology Specialist	Mobile Technology-NFC Study	Wetzikon	Sep 09
Orange	Uwe Raulf	Senior Product Manager	Mobile Technology-NFC Study	Zurich	Sep 09
Swiss	Tiziana Larosa	Business system manager, Marketing, e-business & CRM	Mobile Technology-NFC Study	Kloten	Oct 09
Swiss	Janos Heé	Project Manager e-commerce	Mobile Technology-NFC Study	Kloten	Oct 09
Swiss	Nils Hartgen	Director, Head of direct sales & services	Mobile Technology-NFC Study	Kloten	Oct 09
Starticket	Peter Hürlimann	CEO	Mobile Technology-NFC Study	Zollikon	Nov 09
Cornèr Bank	Giovanni Bettoni	Manager Innovative Solutions	Mobile Technology-NFC Study	Zurich	Oct 09
Visa Europe	Jörg Metzelaers	Country manager CH	Mobile Technology-NFC Study	Zurich	Oct 09
SBB	Andrea Realini	Portfolio Program Manager	Mobile Technology-NFC Study	Berne	Oct 09
Swisscom	Thomas Kummernuss	Residential Customers Customer Experience	Mobile Technology-NFC Study	Zurich	Oct 09

		design			
Ringier AG - Vanilla	Patric G. Baumberger	CEO Vanilla	Mobile Technology- Mobile Payment	Zurich	Jul 10
Ringier AG - Vanilla	Christian Moos	Head Strategic Marketing	Mobile Technology- Mobile Payment	Zurich	Jul 10
Ringier AG	Peter Wolf	Product Manager e-reading	Mobile Technology- Mobile Payment	Zurich	Jul 10

Table 4 Detailed list of interviews.

8.2. Copies of publications

8.2.1. The Crowdsourcing process: an intermediary mediated idea generation approach in the early phase of innovation

Int. J. Entrepreneurship and Innovation Management, Vol. , No. , 2010

The Crowdsourcing process: an intermediary mediated idea generation approach in the early phase of innovation

Louise Muhdi*

Swiss Federal Institute of Technology Zurich (ETHZ), Rämistrasse 101, 8092 Zurich, Switzerland.
E-mail: lmuhdi@ethz.ch

Michael Daiber

University of St.Gallen (HSG), Dufourstrasse 40a, 9000 St. Gallen.
E-Mail: michael.daiber@unisg.ch

Sascha Friesike

University of St.Gallen (HSG), Dufourstrasse 40a, 9000 St. Gallen.
E-Mail: sascha.friesike@unisg.ch

Prof. Dr. Roman Boutellier

Swiss Federal Institute of Technology Zurich (ETHZ), Rämistrasse 101, 8092 Zurich, Switzerland.
E-mail: roman.boutellier@sl.ethz.ch

* Corresponding author

Abstract: Intermediary mediated Crowdsourcing (CS) has become a widely adopted Open Innovation approach for idea generation in various companies of different industries. Despite many success stories and a large body of literature in the fields of idea generation, online competition and open innovation little is known about the intermediary mediated CS process in the early stage of the innovation process. An explorative, qualitative and quantitative multi-case study research design was applied to extract the longitudinal data that were analyzed in this research. Based on twelve CS projects executed by nine Swiss companies from four industries on the Swiss intermediary CS platform atizo.com, five important phases of the intermediary mediated CS process were identified and described. Additionally, important tasks within each phase which ought to be considered by companies when engaging in an intermediary mediated CS project for idea generation were elaborated.

Keywords: Intermediary mediated Crowdsourcing; Open Innovation; idea generation; early innovation phase; online idea competition; explorative longitudinal case studies; Internet enabled innovation; Switzerland.

Reference to this paper should be made as follows: Muhdi, L., Daiber, M., Friesike, S. and Boutellier, R. (2010) 'The Crowdsourcing process: an intermediary mediated idea generation approach in the early phase of innovation', Int. J. Entrepreneurship and Innovation Management, Vol. , No. , pp. .

Biographical notes: Louise Muhdi is a research associate and doctoral candidate at the chair of Technology and Innovation Management at ETH Zurich. Her research focuses on Open Innovation, Crowdsourcing and mobile technologies. She has an MSc in natural sciences from ETH Zurich and has held several national and international management positions in pharmaceutical companies including Serono International Business Operations, Astellas AG and Novo Nordisk.

Michael Daiber is a research associate and doctoral candidate in innovation management at the University of St. Gallen, Switzerland. His research focuses on the integration of external actors into the innovation process and the management of global R&D. He conducted research projects with companies like Airbus, Siemens, Nestlé, Hilti, MAN, Lonza, Liebherr and Henkel. Michael Daiber gained a MSc in Mechanical Engineering from the ETH Zurich with specializations in product development and manufacturing technologies.

Sascha Friesike is a Ph.D. student at the Institute of Technology Management at the University of St.Gallen. He is currently a visiting researcher at Stanford University. He holds an engineering master from the TU Berlin.

Roman Boutellier has been Vice President Human Resources and Infrastructure at ETH Zurich since October 2008. Professor Boutellier has been Chair for Technology and Innovation Management at the Department of Management, Technology and Economics at ETH Zurich since 2004. He has also been titular professor at the University of St. Gallen since 1999. His work has appeared in R&D Management, Harvard Business Manager, ZFO and Drug Discovery Today. He has held several leading positions in the industry.

1 Introduction

During the last decade the propensity to cooperate beyond corporate boundaries and incorporate external knowledge into internal innovations has increased within most companies. Open Innovation describes this phenomenon and has become a topic of great interest to academics and practitioners alike (von Hippel, 1988, Enkel, 2009, Gassmann, 2006, Chesbrough, 2003b, Chesbrough, 2006, Chesbrough, 2003a, Huston, 2006). Today, Open Innovation is a widely accepted remedy against falling prices, offshoring, and innovation races. The significant decrease of transaction costs, the popularity of the Internet and the rapid developments in information and communication technologies (ICTs) have enabled ubiquitous and distributed information generation e.g. Wikipedia, Twitter or Flickr (Surowiecki, 2004). Many companies have leveraged these developments to their own profit by utilizing novel tools, enabling the integration of knowledge of a large number of voluntarily external contributors into the internal innovation process (Gordon, 2008). The term Crowdsourcing (CS), first introduced by Jeff Howe in the Wired magazine (Howe, 2006), is increasingly used to describe this trend and has become one of the most talked about methods of Open Innovation. In its broad definition CS is described as outsourcing tasks traditionally performed by an employee or a contractor to a large group of people or a community (crowd) through an open call online. The contribution of external knowledge is hence made possible by advanced ICTs such as the Internet or mobile phones (Ebner, 2009, Fichter, 2009). In most cases participants have no guaranteed reward. Several papers have described successful practices of CS in various fields such as design, R&D or marketing (Ebner, 2009, Piller, 2006, Kirschbaum, 2005). Literature has as well cited specialized CS intermediaries or virtual knowledge brokers (Verona et al., 2006) such as innocentive.com or ninesigma.com as examples of how modern ICTs have opened up novel possibilities for companies to enrich and, to some extent, modify their conventional innovation processes (Lakhani, 2009, Pisanno, 2008). These intermediaries operate an internet community, collect their information and distribute the information to their customers in order to contribute to their innovation processes. Nowadays, CS is commonly used as a standard approach for idea generation in the early innovation phase (Bonabeau, 2009, Ebner, 2009). The early phase of an innovation process, the so called front-end of new product development, can be defined as the stage of idea generation to the decision for further development (Murphy, 1997). Literature has identified the early phases of innovation to contribute directly to success in product innovation (Dwyer, 1991, Verworn, 2009).

This paper focuses on intermediary mediated CS activities for innovation and idea generation purposes. As idea generation is a major contribution to a successful early phase of innovation processes (Majaro, 1988), these activities have to be taken seriously. Although researchers have investigated and described many Open Innovation approaches there are still limited empirical examinations of the intermediary mediated CS process for idea generation. Especially the question how companies engage in these kinds of processes is still under-researched. Based on the insights of twelve CS from nine Swiss companies we contribute to filling this gap by describing five phases of a CS process and within them the challenges companies often face. In a literature review we first describe existing knowledge on idea generation methods in general and focus specially on CS. We then describe the insights attained from the case studies about the five phases of an intermediary mediated CS process and discuss and compare them to existing literature in a subsequent chapter.

2 Literature review

Creativity is defined by researchers as the production of novel and useful ideas in any domain. Hence, idea generation is an important component of creativity research. Up to this date, various tools and methods have been described in academic literature focusing on idea generation starting with Osborn's book Applied imagination (Osborn, 1953). Since, a large amount of brainstorming literature followed, in particular those describing different types of brainstorming (e.g. nominal or group brainstorming) and their effectiveness (Diehl and Stroebe, 1991, Diehl, 1987, Putman and Paulus, 2009, Brown and Paulus, 2002, Sutton and Hargadon, 1996). Surprisingly, results from numerous experiments led to the findings that the performance of individuals is generally superior to that of groups. The development of computers and IT in general led to an increasing amount of computer supported research, theory and applied work on group creativity. Based on computer stimulations of an associative memory model of idea generation in groups, Brown and Paulus (Brown and Paulus, 2002) argued that group brainstorming can be an effective technique for generating creative ideas. Nijstad and Stroebe (Nijstad and Stroebe, 2006) proposed the SIAM model (Search for Ideas in Associative Memory), which they believe could account for various research findings on group idea generation. Furthermore, advantages and disadvantages of electronic brainstorming compared to conventional face-to-face setting were widely discussed (Dennis, 2004, Dennis, 1993, Dennis, 1999, Gallupe, 1991). In the context of computer-mediated idea generation research was conducted to address related issues such as e.g. group size and anonymity influence (Valacich et al., 1992, Sosik et al., 1998), problem presentation (Dennis et al., 1996), group organization (Dennis and Valacich, 1994) and competition (Munkes and Diehl, 2003). Due to the popularity of the Internet, the developments of evermore sophisticated ICTs and the emergence of a large number of online communities literature about innovation communities, innovation processes, online idea competitions, the role of Open Innovation intermediaries and Crowdsourcing came up.

Different studies focused on the question whether these new methods have benefic effects for the companies. Researchers found that up to 30% of the problems that could not be solved internally found a successful outcome with help of these intermediaries (Lakhani et al., 2006), and that companies could save cost, resources and access more diverse knowledge by cooperating with these intermediaries (Bishop, 2009)

Another main topic treated in literature is the motivation of the participants in online idea competition and the factors that lead to maximizing the idea input. Based on results from open source software development (von Hippel and Von Krogh, 2006, von Krogh and von Hippel, 2006) and the free sharing of information in innovation communities (Franke and Shah, 2003, Jeppesen and Frederiksen, 2006) scholars have investigated the motivation of individuals to contribute to companies' innovation process without a secure reward. Factors contributing to the participant's motivation include the reputation and recognition among peers, the need for improved products. Antikaianen and Ahonen (Antikainen and Ahonen, 2010) claimed that monetary rewards alone are not enough to motivate contributors of innovation communities to participate and collaborate. Intangible factors such as community cooperation, learning and entertainment were shown to be important. Fairness within the CS process and for rewarding has additionally been revealed as a key factor to successfully motivate external contributors to participate in CS projects (Franke and Klausberger, 2009).

These insights play an important role for companies when engaging into CS processes but do not describe which challenges have to be managed in the different parts of a CS project. Ebner's (Ebner, 2009) article gives some insights about this and describes on base of one case study different phases (e.g. idea generation and revision, community evaluation, expert evaluation) of an IT-supported idea competition. Other contributions to online idea competition from practitioner's literature e.g. (Bonabeau, 2009) explain important challenges that have to be overcome in idea generation phase and idea evaluation phase when relying on collective intelligence.

Although not included in a process description different scholars describe important factors that influence the success of a CS project before and after the actual idea competition takes place. As a contribution to the preparation of an idea competition, theoretical literature describes different settings of idea competitions (internal, firm hosted, with intermediary) and in which case to choose one of them (Terwiesch and Xu, 2008). Through case studies from InnoCentive projects Sieg et al. (Sieg et al., 2010) highlight three major challenges that need to be overcome before performing CS with an innovation intermediary: (1) enlisting internal scientists, (2) selecting the right problems, and (3) formulating the R&D problems in order to enable novel solutions.

The challenges that have to be overcome after an idea competition to make use of the results of a project for innovative products and services are less researched. Piller and Walcher (Piller, 2006) show that the results of an idea competition do not directly lead to an innovative product and describe workshops with successful contributors to the competition as a possible subsequent step in order to utilize the competition's best results for innovation purposes. The importance of refining and enriching incoming ideas after they have been evaluated is also described in a case study about a well known CS competition, Cisco's i-Prize (Jouret, 2009)

3 Research design

The literature reviewed in the previous chapters gives insights on different tasks and challenges within an intermediary mediated CS project but do not provide a complete and sequential overview of them. CS projects can be seen as continuous processes that typically require longitudinal observations (Pettigrew, 1990), prompting a case study design. Hence, in order to obtain deeper insight into the intermediary mediated CS process we applied an explorative multi-case study research design (Eisenhardt, 1989, Yin, 2003, Stake, 1995) to extract longitudinal data and performed a qualitative as well as a quantitative analysis of these data. It has recently been argued by Shah and Corley (Shah, 2006) that combined analysis offer valuable insights.

3.1. Case study and CS intermediary selection

Data were collected from 12 individual CS projects performed by 9 Swiss companies from 4 different industries, namely the insurance industry, the banking industry, the energy industry and the tourism industry (Table 1). There were three main reasons for selecting these cases: First, the CS projects are performed by companies from different industries. This allowed us to control and detect environmental variations. Second, we chose to study multiple cases within each industry in order to allow the replication of the findings within the industry group. Third, given the research focus to understand the CS process, we searched for successfully performed CS projects. The criteria for a successful CS project are based on positive answers of the following questions taken from the last round of interviews: 1. Are you generally satisfied with the executed CS project? 2. After having gathered experiences with this intermediary mediated CS project, 2. Would you/your company utilize CS as an approach for idea generation in the future? 3. Will you utilize the results of the performed CS project to integrate in e.g. business plans, in product/service/process development or improvements?

The CS projects were executed on the online platform of the Swiss open innovation intermediary Atizo. Atizo was estimated to be an optimal platform to investigate the CS process as it was an established CS intermediary supporting the idea generation process of various companies and had an online "innovator" community consisting of on average 4'500 heterogeneous members with different backgrounds during 2009.

3.2. Data sources

This study relies on data collected during three rounds of semi-structured interviews conducted with two company participants from each of the 12 CS projects as well as interviews on a weekly basis with Atizo representatives throughout the entire research project duration (the entire year 2009). The interviews were conducted at the following project phases; 1. interview round: shortly before project initiation, 2. interview round: two weeks after the online publication of the CS question and 3. interview round: approximately one month after project termination. The participants were given the opportunities to share their experiences and thoughts, state opinion and narrate stories. In total 72 interviews were conducted and lasted on average 60 min. The interview guidelines for all three interview rounds had some similarities in order to capture possible change. The first interview round included, amongst others, questions regarding the company and its positioning in its industry, its innovation culture, its conventional innovation processes, perceived utility and compatibility of the CS project, motivation, perceived potential/risks and drivers/ inhibitors in connection with the CS project and the online intermediary CS platform. The second interview round included questions regarding e.g. satisfaction with the ongoing CS project, any occurring special issues, expectation towards the CS project and the results, perceived or experienced success/risk factors and drivers/inhibitors. The third interview round included questions revealing the different opinions towards the CS project, lessons learned and future intentions with the achieved results. The CS process phases were identified through parallel comparison of the 3 interview rounds, which were identical for all 12 CS projects. For each answer we identified points of similarities and differences between the 12 CS projects and were able to extract a primary structure of the CS process and its different phases. This scaffold was gradually further developed until all essential details were included and documented leading to the emergence of the detailed intermediary mediated CS process.

3.3. Project details

The questions were posted, and made visible for the innovator community, on Atizo's online platform between April 9th 2009 and September 4th 2009. Depending on the timing, the request of the company and advice of Atizo the questions were online for a total duration of 6-10 weeks (Table 1). The community was restricted by Atizo to submit contributions containing a maximum of 150 words and one image. However, rating and commenting tools were available to community members and companies for utilization during the idea generation phase. Table 1 illustrates that different amounts of ideas were submitted to each CS project and on average more than 260 ideas were generated within 6 to 10 weeks.

Table 1 Detailed list of the CS projects conducted during this research.

Company name	Industry	Project name	Weeks online	# of ideas
Helsana	Health insurance	Sales of health insurance online	8	212
Helsana	Health insurance	Creation of an online campaign for Helsana	8	165
KPT	Health insurance	New services: The online health platform	6	291
PostFinance	Banking	Creative ways to approach customers (in financial services)	8	248
PostFinance	Banking	Attractive online-services for Post Finance customers	8	269
KWRO	Tourism	Raising awareness about accident risks in ski-regions	7	339
SBB mobiliar	Tourism	Customer friendly large train stations	7	490
Graubünden	Tourism	Community website Graubünden	8	365
ewb	Energy	Innovative energy provider	6	315
ewb	Energy	Individually mobile: Energy from the power socket	9	428
youtility	Energy	Gas products for households and small businesses	6	196
Bühler	Energy	Business model for energy consulting	10	177

4 Findings

The twelve case studies have delivered insights contributing to the overall understanding of how intermediary mediated CS works for idea generation in the early innovation process. The findings and recommendations are directed towards companies which are interested in utilizing the virtual CS approach to generate ideas in the early innovation processes. As a result of this research, five phases of the CS process were identified to be important (Figure 1): 1. The deliberation phase, 2. The preparation phase, 3. The execution phase, 4. The assessment phase, and 5. The post-processing phase. All phases are elaborated in the following sections.

Figure 1 Five important phases of the intermediary mediated CS process.

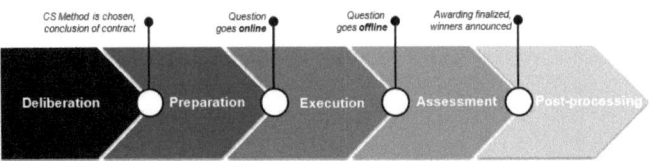

Phase 1: Deliberation

The deliberation phase describes the initial period of a CS process. This phase begins when a company shows interest in the CS approach in order to tackle ongoing challenges.

EWB, for example, realized the growing potential of the electro mobility market in the latest years and have been searching for innovative ways to gain access to this market. Since idea generation can be achieved by different means, companies must evaluate different approaches matching their needs during this phase. In short, here companies have to decide whether the CS approach is appropriate to solve their internal problem/problems.

1. Overall analysis of the CS approach

Initially, the companies tried to attain an in-depth understanding of the CS process in order to estimate the potential benefits and risks of CS for the company. Hence, important information, such as the exact course of a CS project (e.g. method, approach), the virtual CS platform (e.g. structure, set-up), intermediaries (e.g. scope, strengths, networks) and community profile (e.g. number of members, profile distribution (e.g. gender, age, profession, interests), were collected and evaluated. Much of this information is commonly provided by an experienced intermediary during acquisition. However, in order to complete the initial set of information additional internal investigations were made and estimated crucial. Information collected during this phase supported the decision as to whether or not a CS approach is compatible with existing internal processes and is in alignment with company values. Questions such as "How is the appearance of the CS platform?", "Which other companies have used the intermediary CS platform for idea generation in the past?", and "Is the CS platform user-friendly?" formed the companies perceptions towards the CS approach.

2. Reflection on how internal problems can be approached with the CS approach

Beyond direct project costs (intermediary fees, rewards, etc.), various internal resources (e.g. internal labor costs) were attached to the execution of the CS project. These additional efforts and investments were initially underestimated. Hence, companies found it important to thoroughly reflect on whether the CS approach can create a considerable added value by solving internal problems.

3. Promote internal buy-in

Some companies realized that much effort is needed to overcome internal inertia, also known as the not invented here syndrome (Katz, 1982), and achieve internal buy-in for a CS project. Buy-in, in this context, means to convince a group of internal people rather than only one person who says yes to an idea, a plan, a step, or a project. Findings indicated that failing this task can jeopardize the success of an entire CS project by delaying or inhibiting the implementation of the outcome ideas.

The deliberation phase of the CS process is terminated when the decision is made about whether or not to conclude a contract with a CS intermediary.

Phase 2: Preparation

The preparation phase begins subsequent to the conclusion of a contract with an intermediary for a CS project. It describes the necessary groundwork that must be accomplished prior to the initiation of the online idea generation. The following seven points emerged in our research as being important in the preparation phase of a CS process:

1. Clarification of company expectations towards the CS project

Once the internal commitment to carry out a CS project was achieved, expectations of companies towards the CS procedure as well as the outcome (e.g. number of ideas generated and quality of the generated ideas) were clarified. Done properly, this step has shown to decreases the risk of possible future disappointments and misunderstandings. Evidence from our case studies revealed that a source of experience and expertise in CS can be helpful to match company expectations and the realistic possibilities of CS. In our research, the intermediary had a reference-list, was in possession of required expertise, and insights were also provided by an external CS consultant. At the beginning of their CS project, Helsana, having no previous experience with the CS approaches, expected break through ideas to be generated. The guidance provided by the CS intermediary and the CS consultant helped Helsana in adjusting their outcome expectations to a more realistic level and to continue the project building on the achieved insight.

2. Definition of a question fitting to the CS approach

A central task in the preparation phase of the CS process is the definition and the accurate formulation of the CS question. Our research showed the importance of clarifying which outcome is expected or which goal is aimed at before defining the question. Since the outcomes can be of various natures, the companies had to clarify whether they were looking for ideas regarding innovative products, processes or services or a community opinion regarding a certain theme, or for confirmations of internal ideas or intentions. Furthermore, results confirmed that reputational impacts must be carefully planned and well reflected upon in advance to avoid unexpected or negative external influence.

3. Formulation of the question's exact wording.

When the problem is discussed and defined internally its formulation must be carefully thought through as changes are no longer possible after putting the question online. Once the formulation is finalized and the question is published, the CS community will submit solutions according to their understanding of the question. Differences between the understanding of the question within the company and the community can lead to rather unsatisfactory outcome.

Our research indicated that defining the exact wording is the most challenging task and requires much experience, intuition and methodology. Hence, the collaboration with CS experts for the formulation of the question can improve the outcome considerably. This problem was found to be done best in a way that enhances lateral thinking (De Bono, 1990) within a heterogeneous idea provider community. Questions packed with too much precise information were often misunderstood and answered fuzzily, a fact known from research in creativity (March, 1999). According to Atizo, keeping the questions simple enough for anyone to read and understand by keeping them short (restrictions are therefore often given by intermediaries) and delimited to one aim only, is of advantage. Another approach to improve the formulation of the CS question is to integrate internal people with different expertise and background in this task as it was done by PostFinance. Here, a communication specialist, different project managers, and a CS consultant participated in the meetings to agree upon the wording of the question.

4. Reflection on timing of the CS project and the online duration of the question

Following the finalization and approval of the CS question, the timing of the publication on the intermediary platform and the duration of the idea generation must be addressed. The questions in our case studies were online for 6-10 weeks. Our research showed that the highest response rate was achieved in the first week after the questions were published online (Figure 2). This was followed by a relatively slow accumulation of submitted ideas during the following weeks. Data showed that 63-87 % of the ideas in the CS projects were generated within the first 4 weeks (Figure 3).

Figure 2 Accumulated number of ideas generated vs. duration of the CS question online (an example including two CS projects).

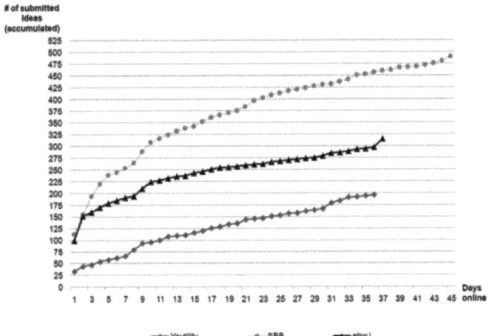

A prolongation of the time period for idea generation did not have a direct relation to the total number of ideas generated. A comparison of the number of ideas submitted within each project after 28 days indicated that the number of submitted ideas is not a direct function of the duration the question is online (Figure 3). The community activity varied between the different CS projects, which leads to our assumption that other factors are most probably responsible for the differences. These could include the topic, the timing, and the formulation of the question. We suggest addressing these topics in further research.

Figure 3 Number of ideas generated vs. duration of the CS question online.

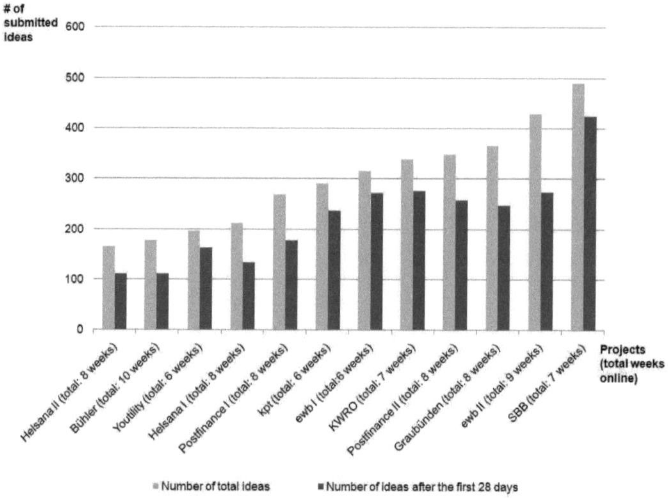

5. Definition of the idea rating criteria

A set of idea rating criteria were defined, posted online and thereby made visible for the community members. KPT, for example, defined the following criteria for their CS project: 1) the idea provides added value for KPT customers, 2) the idea is innovative (service innovation), and 3) The idea fits the image of the online health insurer KPT. On one hand, these idea rating criteria facilitated the later rating process of the submitted ideas and served, on the other hand, as project guidelines for the community members to rely upon. This task was found to simplify the later evaluation process.

6. Planning internal resources

To ensure an optimal execution of the CS project, the persons or teams involved in the CS project were informed about their responsibilities, provided with necessary information, and introduced to the appropriate tools. This proved to be an important task to ensure optimal time management of the involved internal employees during project execution.

7. Reflection on strategies to increase the participation in own CS project.

In order to increase the number of active community members, several companies e.g. KPT, Helsana and PostFinance chose to inform selected colleagues or all company employees about the ongoing CS project. According to Atizo, the visibility and participation of persons in possession of useful knowledge in the CS project can be increased by integrating a project link, with the purpose of spreading information about the ongoing project, on other existing virtual platforms such as the social network platforms like facebook.com, interest blogs or online forums. However, the success rate can vary depending on the nature of the approached communities. If a company aims to achieve highly innovative ideas it can be worth considering integrating communities with individuals in possession of different backgrounds and interests rather than the typical experts with whom the company would usually work with.

Phase 3: Execution

The execution phase is the third phase of the CS process. This phase begins when the CS question is posted online and thereby made visible to the virtual CS community. In this phase community members are encouraged to submit ideas fitting the question published. The execution phase ends when the question goes offline. The following two tasks were found important in this phase:

1. Gradually reading and possibly clustering the received ideas.

While idea generation is ongoing, companies are limited in their actions. However, one essential task for companies is to progressively read all ideas as they are received. To increase the project overview and monitor the progress of the CS project, an early clustering of the received ideas has shown to be useful.

A rough classification helped the early identification of trends and assisted the following idea rating process. For this task tools were offered by the intermediary Atizo.

2. Communication with community members

During idea generation, companies were able to communicate with selected community members. Queries were forwarded to some idea providers and chosen ideas were commented on by some of the participating companies. By investing two hours per week on commenting received ideas and answering community questions, Youtility reported that they managed to obtain deeper insights on potential customers' expectations and fears related to gas products. Atizo made it possible for companies to label interesting ideas which then were visible to the community members. This labeling function was thought to function as a community guide as well.

Phase 4: Assessment

The assessment phase begins when idea generation is terminated and the CS question is taken offline. In this stage the submitted ideas are clustered, rated and best ideas are rewarded. Due to the relatively high number of ideas generated, it has shown to be important to use proven tools for evaluation.

1. Tool selection for clustering and rating of received ideas

Three IT tools designed to facilitate the clustering/categorization and the idea rating of the received ideas were offered to the participating companies by the intermediary Atizo:

- Exporting tool: allows export of submitted ideas straight from the Atizo platform in any preferred format such as e.g. MS Excel or PDF for further assessment and analysis.

- Online idea rating tool/pre-screening: allows the online rating of submitted ideas in a rating scale of 1 (poor) to 5 (excellent). Furthermore, it allows the client to add labeling comments to each idea. This facilitates subsequent categorization and identification of best ideas.
- Mind mapping tool: MindMaster is a user-friendly online mind mapping tool which allows exporting desired ideas directly from atizo.com to MindMaster where they can be categorized according to chosen criteria or preferences.

2. Definition of an internal rating strategy

Depending on the internal conditions and preferences, the involved companies defined individual idea rating strategies. The strategies were diverse and differed in the choice of assessors: who performs the rating, according to which categories, and when does it take place. It was shown to be advantageous if more than one company internal employee rated the submitted ideas according to preset criteria and classified them according to previously defined categories. Our research indicates that a discussion based on the different rating results improved and assisted the identification of prime ideas.

3. Rewarding best idea/ideas

The rewards were either distributed to one idea only or to several ideas. The rewarding strategies varied from project to project. However, it is known that sharing rewards amongst several community members can result in an increase of motivation of the community members. Due to the fact that Atizo publishes the names of the winners on their online platform, some companies chose to rewards multiple ideas rather than one in order to prevent competitors from gaining information about future implementation strategies. However, this was not the main objective as many companies had the desire to encourage community members for possible future collaboration.

Phase 5: Post-processing

The final phase of the intermediary mediated CS process is the post-processing phase. This phase begins when best ideas, generated through the CS approach, have been identified and rewarded. All companies participating in this research communicated that they intend to integrate the overall results (e.g. selected ideas, trends, a combination of complementary ideas, etc.) in existing or future project. In order to leverage the results achieved through the CS project, companies stressed the importance of an implementation plan and the management of the side effects as follows:

1. Interpretation of the results and planning their implementation

In this phase, the overall results of the CS project were interpreted in the context of the company and implementation strategies were sought for. Depending on the nature of the results, they were planned to be incorporated into existing projects as an add-on to existing ideas from the conventional innovation process or should lead to the initiation of novel projects. EWB, for example, stated that their business plans for entering the electro mobility market were influenced by the CS project results, either by confirming internal intentions or adapting them.

2. Management of side-effects

Some results of the CS projects often had the potential to be useful, for instance in other departments within the company. In order to promote these positive side effects, interesting ideas were communicated and forwarded internally after termination of the CS project.

Figure 4 is a simplified overview of the overall results of this research. This figure illustrates the identified five phases of the intermediary mediated CS process and their important tasks.

Figure 4 Five phases and important tasks in the CS process.

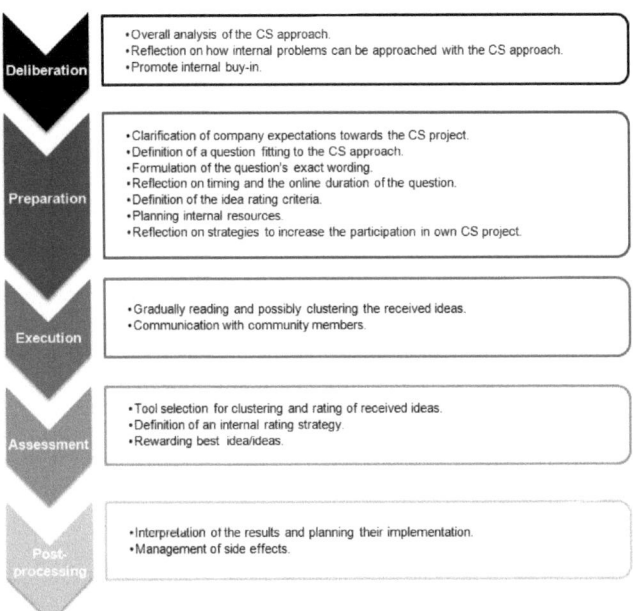

5 Discussion

The phenomena of open innovation combined with the possibilities provided by the Internet have opened up novel possibilities for idea generation and innovation.

While previous literature has described various methods, processes and challenges (Sosik et al., 1998, Munkes and Diehl, 2003, Dennis et al., 1996, Osborn, 1953, Paulus and Yang, 2000, Brown and Paulus, 2002, Valacich et al., 1992) related to traditional idea generation performed within the company boundaries, recent literature describes rather open and virtual idea generation processes and methods such as CS allowing the sourcing of information and knowledge from virtual communities composed of people with different backgrounds and interests (Bonabeau, 2009). On the basis of a literature review in the fields of open innovation, idea generation and idea completion as well as a multiple-case study we have provided an in depth description of the entire intermediary mediated CS process for idea generation and insights about tasks to be considered in order to improve the overall success rate. Different phases of a CS project have earlier been described, i.e. in Ebner's article (Ebner, 2009), however not as detailed as in our paper and not with an intermediary. We contribute to the literature by describing the process starting from the point where companies consider utilizing this new open innovation approach for problem solving to the time where the CS results are extracted and elements are planned for implementation or integration within the company. Moreover, we elaborated on challenges throughout the process and make suggestions how to overcome those. We found the tasks in the first two phases (deliberation and preparation) to be particularly decisive for the success of a CS project due to the virtual and open innovation context. The decisions made here are definitive and cannot be corrected in later phases unlike e.g. during a traditional idea generation workshop where a closed group of people meet physically. Challenges in these phases have to a certain extent been described in other publications. Terwiesch and Xu (Terwiesch and Xu, 2008) for example described companies' choice between different types of idea competitions and Sieg et al. (Sieg et al., 2010) addressed challenges to be considered before performing CS. Additionally we emphasize on the importance of the activities after idea evaluation (post-processing). Since the results are generated externally an additional effort for interpretation and implementation into the company's context is essential. Also here only few articles have given hints on how to transform results from an online idea competition into innovative products or services (Piller, 2006). Further literature is however expected addressing this issue since innovation is only occurring when the transformation of ideas or results into products/services take place.

6 Conclusion

In this research we identified and described the CS process to be composed of five phases and emphasized important tasks within each phase, which ought to be considered when engaging in a CS project. Our research adds generally to the idea generation and online idea competition literature and more precisely to the limited empirical examinations about intermediary mediated CS by providing insight into how companies engage in these processes and which challenges they face during the different phases. Business professionals can utilize the insights of this paper to improve their understanding of the process underlying intermediary enabled virtual CS. In-depth understanding of the different phases and the associated tasks, the advantages and the limitations of the CS process can improve its application for idea generation and decision making support within the company. The findings can assist optimizing investigation how to implement CS in early innovation processes.

Limitations and implications for further research

Further research in the implementation phase of the achieved CS results can provide valuable insight about the success rate of the CS projects in different companies. In this context, interesting insights could be how and in which form the achieved results are incorporated within the companies. Moreover, it is valuable to understand which factors influence the quality of the virtually generated ideas and its results. Some interesting issues that should be investigated are the effect of e.g. the type of online community on idea generation and factors that motivate and support community members to collaborate in an Open Innovation setting.

7 Acknowledgment

This research was supported by the CTI (Swiss Innovation Promotion Agency). The authors wish to thank all case study partners for their time as well as the University of Applied Sciences Western Switzerland (HES-SO) for providing the data of the following case studies: KWRO, SBB mobiliar, and Graubünden.

8 References

ANTIKAINEN, M. & AHONEN, M. (2010) Motivating and supporting collaboration in open innovation. European Journal of Innovation Management, 13, 100-119.

BISHOP, M. (2009) The Total Economic Impact of InnoCentive Challenges. Cambridge, MA, Forrester Consulting.

BONABEAU, E. (2009) Decisions 2.0: The Power of Collective Intelligence. MIT Sloan Management Review, 50, 45-+.

BROWN, V. R. & PAULUS, P. B. (2002) Making group brainstorming more effective: Recommendations from an associative memory perspective. Current Directions in Psychological Science, 11, 208-212.

CHESBROUGH, H. W. (2003a) The era of Open Innovation. Sloan Management Review, 44, 35-41.

CHESBROUGH, H. W. (2003b) Open innovation the new imperative for creating and profiting from technology, Boston, MA, Harvard Business School Press.

CHESBROUGH, H. W. (2006) Open innovation researching a new paradigm, Oxford, Oxford University Press.

DE BONO, E. (1990) Lateral thinking for management, London, Penguin Books.

DENNIS, A. R., AND REINICKE, B. A. (2004) BETA versus VHS and the acceptance of electronic brainstorming technology. MIS Quarterly, 28.

DENNIS, A. R., AND VALACICH, J. S. (1993) Computer brainstorming: More heads are better than one. Journal of Applied Psychology, 78, 513-537.

DENNIS, A. R., AND VALACICH, J. S. (1999) Research note. electronic brainstorming: Illusions and patterns of productivity. Information Science Research, 10, 375-377.

DENNIS, A. R. & VALACICH, J. S. (1994) Group, subgroup, and nominal group idea generation - new rules for a new media Journal of Management, 20, 723-736.

DENNIS, A. R., VALACICH, J. S., CONNOLLY, T. & WYNNE, B. E. (1996) Process structuring in electronic brainstorming. Information Systems Research, 7, 268-277.

DIEHL, M., AND STROEBE, W. (1987) Productivity loss in brainstorming groups - towards the solution of a riddle. Journal of Personality and Social Psychology, 53, 497-509.

DIEHL, M. & STROEBE, W. (1991) Productivity loss in idea-generating groups - tracking down the blocking effect Journal of Personality and Social Psychology, 61, 392-403.

DWYER, L., AND MELLOR, R. (1991) Organizational environment, new product process activities, and project outcomes. Journal of Product Innovation Management, 8, 39-48.

EBNER, W., LEIMEISTER, J. M, ET AL. (2009) Community engineering for innovation: the ideas competition as a method to nurture a virtual community for innovation. R&D Management, 39, 342-356.

EISENHARDT, K. M. (1989) Building Theories from Case Study Research. Academy of Management Review. Academy of Management.

ENKEL, E., GASSMANN, O, ET AL. (2009) Open R&D and open innovation; exploring the phenomena. R&D Management, 39, 311-316.

FICHTER, K. (2009) Innovation communities; the role of networks in Open Innovation. R&D Management, 39, 357-371.

FRANKE, N. & KLAUSBERGER, K. (2009) The role of percieved fairness in company-centered crwodsourcing communities. Vienna, Vienna University of Economics and Business Administration.

FRANKE, N. & SHAH, S. (2003) How communities suport innovation activities: an exploration of assistance and sharing among end-users. Research Policy, 32, 157 - 178.

GALLUPE, R. H., BASTIANUTTI, H. L, ET AL. (1991) Unblocking brainstorming. Journal of Applied Psychology, 76, 137-142.

GASSMANN, O. (2006) Opening up the innovation process: towards an agenda. R&D Management, 36, 223-228.

GORDON, S., MONIDEEPA, T, ET AL. (2008) Improving the front end of innovation with information technology. Research Technology Management, 51, 50-58.

HOWE, J. (2006) The rise of Crowdsourcing. Wired Magazine.

HUSTON, L., SAKKAB, N. (2006) Connect and develop: Inside Procter & Gamble's new model for innovation. Harvard business review 84, 58.

JEPPESEN, L. B. & FREDERIKSEN, L. (2006) Why do users contribute to firm-hostes user communities? The case of computer-controlled music instruments. Organization Science, 17, 45-63.

JOURET, G. (2009) Inside cisco's Search for the Next Big Idea. Harvard Business Review, 87, 43-45.

KATZ, E., AND ALLEN, T. (1982) Investigating the Not Invented Here Syndrome. R&D Management, 12, 7-19.

KIRSCHBAUM, R. (2005) Open Innovation in Practice. Research-Technology Management, 48, 24-38.

LAKHANI, K. L., BOUDREAU, K. J. (2009) How to manage outside innovation. MIT Sloan Management Review, 50, 69-76.

LAKHANI, K. L., JEPPESEN, L. B., LOHSE, P. A. & PANETTA, J. A. (2006) The value of openness in scientific problem solving. Harvard Business School.

MAJARO, S. (1988) Managing ideas for profits, London, McGraw-Hill.

MARCH, J. G. (1999) The pursuit of organizational intelligence, Malden, Blackwell Business.

MUNKES, J. & DIEHL, M. (2003) Matching or competition? Performance comparison processes in an idea generation task. Group Processes & Intergroup Relations, 6, 305-320.

MURPHY, S. A., AND KUMER, V. (1997) The front end of new product development: a Canadian survey. R&D Management, 27, 5-15.

NIJSTAD, B. A. & STROEBE, W. (2006) How the group affects the mind: A cognitive model of idea generation in groups. Personality and Social Psychology Review, 10, 186-213.

OSBORN, A. (1953) Applied imagination: Principles and procedures of creative problem solving., New York, Charles Screiber's Sons.

PAULUS, P. B. & YANG, H. C. (2000) Idea generation in groups: A basis for creativity in organizations. Organizational Behavior and Human Decision Processes, 82, 76-87.

PETTIGREW, A. M. (1990) Longitudinal Field Research on Change: Theory and Practice. Organization Science, 1, 267-292.

PILLER, F. T., AND WALCHER, D. (2006) Toolkits for idea competitions. a novel method to integrate users in new product development. R&D Management, 307-318.

PISANNO, G. P., AND VERGANTI, R. (2008) Which kind of collaboration is right for you? Harvard Business Review, 86, 78-86.

PUTMAN, V. L. & PAULUS, P. B. (2009) Brainstorming, Brainstorming Rules and Decision Making. Journal of Creative Behavior, 43, 23-39.

SHAH, S. K., AND CORLEY, K.G. (2006) Building better theory by bridging the quantitative-qualitative divide. Journal of Management Studies, 43, 1821-1835.

SIEG, J. H., WALLIN, M. W. & VON KROGH, G. (2010) Managerial challenges in open innovation: a study of innovation intermediation in the chemical industry. R&D Management, 40, 281 - 291.

SOSIK, J. J., AVOLIO, B. J. & KAHAI, S. S. (1998) Inspiring group creativity - Comparing anonymous and identified electronic brainstorming. Small Group Research, 29, 3-31.

STAKE, R. E. (1995) The art of case study research, Thousand Oaks, California [etc.], Sage Publications.

SUROWIECKI, J. (2004) The wisdom of crowds why the many are smarter than the few and how collective wisdom shapes business, economies, societies, and nations, London, Little.

SUTTON, R. I. & HARGADON, A. (1996) Brainstorming groups in context: Effectiveness in a product design firm. Administrative Science Quarterly, 41, 685-718.

TERWIESCH, C. & XU, Y. (2008) Innovation Contests, Open Innovation, and Multiagent Problem Solving. Management Science, 54, 1529 - 1543.

VALACICH, J. S., DENNIS, A. R. & NUNAMAKER, J. F. (1992) GROUP-SIZE AND ANONYMITY EFFECTS ON COMPUTER-MEDIATED IDEA GENERATION. Small Group Research, 23, 49-73.

VERONA, G., PRANDELLI, E. & SAWHNEY, M. (2006) Innovation and virtual environments: Towards virtual knowledge brokers. Organization Studies, 27, 765-788.

VERWORN, B. (2009) A structural equation model of the impact of the "fuzzy front end" on the success of new product development. Research Policy, 38, 1571-1581.

VON HIPPEL, E. (1988) The sources of innovation, New York [etc.], Oxford University Press.

VON HIPPEL, E. & VON KROGH, G. (2006) Free revealing and the private-collective model for innovation incentives R&D Management, 36, 295 - 306.

VON KROGH, G. & VON HIPPEL, E. (2006) The promise of research on open source software. Management Science, 52, 975 - 983.

YIN, R. K. (2003) Case study research design and methods, Thousand Oaks, Sage Publications.

8.2.2. Crowdsourcing for "Kiosk of the Future" - A Retail Store Case Study

Crowdsourcing for "Kiosk of the Future" – A Retail Store Case Study

Erica Dubach Spiegler
ETH Zürich, Department of
Management, Technology and Economics,
Scheuchzerstrasse 7, 8092 Zürich, Switzerland
edubach@ethz.ch

Louise Muhdi
ETH Zürich, Department of
Management, Technology and Economics,
Scheuchzerstrasse 7, 8092 Zürich, Switzerland
lmuhdi@ethz.ch

Dominic Stöcklin
Goldbach Interactive (Switzerland) AG
Mattenstrasse 90, 2503 Biel, Switzerland
dominic.stoecklin@goldbachinteractive.ch

Florian Michahelles
ETH Zürich, Department of
Management, Technology and Economics,
Scheuchzerstrasse 7, 8092 Zürich, Switzerland
fmichahelles@ethz.ch

ABSTRACT

This article reports on a case study which describes how Valora Retail, the company that operates the majority of Kiosks in Switzerland, successfully completed a intermediary mediated Crowdsourcing project as well as the results they achieved using this open innovation approach to generate ideas for the internal project named the "Kiosk of the Future". Out of the 626 ideas virtually submitted by the crowdsourcing community, 64 ideas were evaluated to be relevant for the project and the 19 best ideas were given rewards and were considered for further internal analysis and development. This case study details the process by which the top ideas were chosen and clearly demonstrates a successful application of Crowdsourcing for idea generation for the early innovation process. It was reported that the achieved outcome of this project would unlikely have originated from the company itself due to high internal barriers.

Keywords:

Crowdsourcing, Small-Space Retail, Retail, Open Innovation, Case Study.

INTRODUCTION

Traditionally, innovation took place in a protected and closed environment within large research and development (R&D) departments of companies. Today however, the collaboration with external actors such as business partners, customers and lead users is increasingly accepted to play an important role in companies' innovation capability. Thus, companies are increasingly and actively allowing bi-directional flow of knowledge between the company and the outside of the company. Chesbrough captured and explained this development under the term Open Innovation (OI) (Chesbrough 2003; Enkel, Gassmann 2004). The term Crowdsourcing (CS) was introduced in 2006 (Howe 2006) and can be understood as a subset of OI in which the contribution of external knowledge is facilitated by advanced information and communication technologies (ICTs) such as the internet (Ebner 2009; Fichter 2009). Today, Internet enabled CS is an increasingly used OI approach for idea generation in the early innovation process by many companies from various industries. The popularity of CS is due mainly to two factors: First, the last decade's rapid advancements in novel ICTs, such as the improvement of online communication tools and development of enhanced features for online interaction, have contributed immensely to the adoption and popularity of CS. Second, given the virtual nature of CS, companies are provided with the unique opportunity to benefit from the distributed knowledge of a considerable pool of individuals with different interests and backgrounds (Howe 2008).

The motivations of companies to run CS projects are manifold. Besides being a trendy alternative approach to feed the innovation process to achieve strategic goals, companies often choose this OI approach to e.g. track trends, meet customer needs, obtain an external perspective or achieve confirmation of their own business intentions. The combination of motivations is often dependent on the company, the department, the internal strategy, the industry and the situation.

This article describes a case study showing the utilization of CS in the early innovation process in the company Valora Retail which runs the majority of kiosks in Switzerland under the brand "k Kiosk". Kiosks are small-space retail shops at busy locations and sell convenience products – mainly press, cigarettes, candy, drinks and lottery – to a mass customer base. The current Swiss kiosk business model is projected to run into difficulties for the following reasons: 1) press products are increasingly affected by the digitization of media, 2) cigarettes are subjected to an increase in legislation and bans, 3) candy and sugary drinks are harder purchases to justify in the larger trend towards a healthier life style and, 4) gambling is increasingly moving online. In order to counter these developments which represent severe threats, several internal discussions and workshops were held in autumn 2008. The conclusion was reached that the search for the future role of Kiosks in an increasingly digital world needed to be identified. Since a big part of the threat to the current business comes from the Internet and Web 2.0 based innovations, it was decided internally to use the internet enabled CS approach to gather ideas about what the "Kiosk of the Future" should look like.

In this paper we will describe how Valora Retail successfully completed the CS process – facilitated by an intermediary – and the results they achieved using this OI approach to generate ideas for the "Kiosk of the Future". The structure of the paper is as follows: section 2 describes related work. Section 3 describes the methodology followed by section 4 which describes the step by step results of the CS process as applied by Valora Retail. The discussion will follow in section 5.

Related Work

CS is often utilized as a complementary approach next to the traditional idea generation approaches such as e.g. Brainstorming (Diehl 1987) and TRIZ (Altshuller 1996); however, by basing their entire business model on this popular phenomenon, a number of creative startups have shown that CS by itself can as well lead to success (e.g. threadless.com, istockphoto.com). Regardless if utilized to feed R&D (e.g. Innocentive, NineSigma), marketing (e.g. Guerra Creativa), design (e.g. Jovoto, Burdastyle), idea generation (e.g. fiat Mio, BMW Customer Innovation Lab) or collective intelligence (Wikipedia, Yahoo answers), CS has contributed to solving many challenging problems and enabled many innovations (Ebner 2009, Piller 2006). The intermediary facilitated CS process which is described in detail in this paper, consists of the following five successive phases (Muhdi et al 2010):

1. Within the deliberation phase the companies decide whether or not the CS approach is suitable for solving an internal problem. Furthermore, the internal buy-in is as well an important issue to be achieved. This phase terminates when a contract is concluded with a chosen CS intermediary.

2. All the necessary activities needed to be accomplished before the problem is represented to the solving community of the CS intermediary are executed in the preparation phase. Tasks in this phase include amongst others the clarification of internal expectations towards the CS project and the outcome, exact formulation and presentation of the problem, planning of necessary resources and the timing of the CS project. This phase has a direct impact on the outcome because once the question/problem is online there are no further possibilities to make any changes to the published content.

3. The execution phase describes the time frame where the problem solving community can submit solutions, namely the idea generation phase.
4. In the assessment phase submitted ideas/solutions are evaluated and the best idea providers rewarded.
5. Once the best idea/ideas are identified according to preset criteria the largest part of the work load in the CS process remains – namely the implementation of best idea/ideas. In the post-processing phase companies develop implementation strategies and prepare incorporation of the ideas generated by CS in the innovation process of the company.

Methodology

Valora Retail chose a Swiss CS intermediary company with experience in the Swiss retail market, Atizo, to perform their CS project (www.atizo.com). The company runs a web-based CS platform with a community of 6'400 members at the time of the case study who contribute (Galli 2010). These members generate 40 ideas per day (Atizo 2010) and are situated globally, though most of them are Swiss, followed by people living in Germany, Austria, India and France. The Valora Retail idea generation (execution phase) was conducted on this CS intermediary platform and took 7 weeks (from 21.1.2010 to 16.3.2010), generating 626 ideas. The entire process of all five CS steps is described below.

Results

In this section we will step through the CS process performed by Valora Retail and elaborate the activities and results along the process described above.

Deliberation Phase

The key decision makers for the CS project were the head of process and project management and the head of the "Kiosk of the Future" initiative, both of whom reported to the CEO of Valora Retail. They selected two people to form the operational team for the CS project (CS project team): a team member of the Valora Retail "Strategic Marketing" department and an outside consultant.

Initially the motivation for Valora Retail to start a CS project was three-fold: 1) It is known that there is no "typical" Kiosk customer, as they cut across all demographic categories. A public call for ideas via The CS intermediary company was therefore deemed the best way to achieve a set of ideas with highest diversity. 2) As part of the Kiosk strategy to become more involved in Web 2.0 technologies, initiating a CS project would provide valuable experience in the Web 2.0 domain. 3) The CS participants would provide a first base for a Kiosk internet community interested in and dedicated to the company.

An analysis showed that the third motivation point would require a custom-built platform and offers were solicited for this approach. However, upon inspection Valora Retail decided that the costs were prohibitive and that point was dropped. So instead of relying on a single community to generate ideas which would then transition to be a community for marketing activities, two separate communities were used: 1) A Facebook "Fan page" was launched for marketing activities which focused on the Valora private label products under the brand "ok.-" (www.facebook.com/okPunktStrich), and 2) Atizo, the CS intermediary platform, was chosen because of their existing community of innovators which were a good fit with the type of "Web 2.0 customers" that Valora Retail wanted to understand better.

This split reduced any development risks and so the project could easily be budgeted. The combination of a more controlled process thanks to outsourcing the CS and compensating for the lack of community by setting up the Facebook Fan Page, convinced Valora Retail senior management to approve the CS project.

Preparation Phase

The initial step in the preparation phase of the CS process was the definition of the company's expectations towards the CS project. Valora Retail's expectations were on the one hand to gain first experiences with an idea generation approach based on Web 2.0, and on the other hand to generate surprising ideas which probably would not be proposed by internal committees and from workshops with experts.

The overarching strategic goal of the "Kiosk of the Future" project was to find ways to combine the physical Kiosk retail spaces – which are one of the main assets of Valora Retail – with information available online to gain business and strategic advantages in the future. In order to achieve this goal, the CS question was formulated as follows: : "The Kiosk with its many locations will become the hub between the physical and digital world. Which surprising ideas, products and services can you imagine in the context of the Kiosk of the Future?"(In the original German: «Der Kiosk mit seinen vielen Standorten soll Schnittstelle zwischen realer und digitaler Welt sein. Welche überraschenden Ideen, Produkte und Services können Sie sich rund um den Kiosk der Zukunft vorstellen?»).

The CS question was drafted by the CS project team and tested by internal employees. Furthermore, the CS intermediary company also reviewed the CS question to ensure that the intended message was being conveyed preventing community misunderstandings or incorrect interpretations.

In parallel to drafting the CS question, the evaluation criteria that would be used to rank the ideas were defined. These were published on the CS platform alongside the CS question and were visible to the innovator community:

- The degree of interaction between the Kiosk products and Web 2.0
- The level of appeal (attractiveness) for a broad customer base
- The value of information and entertainment

The CS question was published on the CS intermediary company platform as soon as it was technically possible in order to accelerate the CS project time line. The duration of the idea gathering was set to 7 weeks, following the recommendation given by the CS intermediary company.

Subsequent to the publication of the CS question, As soon as the question was online, the CS project team used their networks within Valora Retail and an academic institution respectively, to announce the CS activity in an effort to increase participation. Furthermore, personal networks such as Twitter and Facebook accounts were activated as well by posting the link to the CS project.

Finally in the preparation phase, the CS project team planned their resources for the upcoming execution and evaluation phases. Since the CS tasks were to be performed on top of daily business, the CS project team anticipated and accepted an increase in work load.

Execution Phase

Over the course of the 7 weeks in which the CS project ran, 626 ideas were generated, which significantly exceeded the expectations of Valora Retail. The first week saw the largest number of ideas submitted (233 ideas, or 37.2% of the total), but a steady stream continued during the following 6 weeks until conclusion (see Fig. 1).

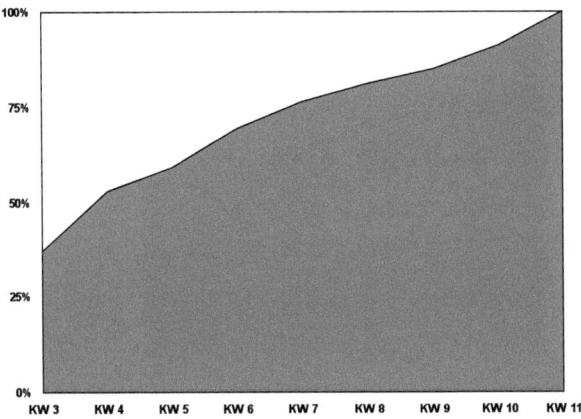

Figure 1: Number of ideas generated by week

As is characteristic for the crowdsourcing process, the ideas arrived in no particular order and in a very wide range of quality, meaning that both the quality and length of the idea text varied, as well as the quality of the idea content. In general it can be stated that the ideas displayed a wide breadth, i.e. a wide range of ideas that had never occurred to the retail professionals at Valora Retail or the IT specialists supporting them.

At the start of the project, the CS team had decided to use the ranking system which the CS intermediary company provides as a standard for both innovators and moderators since it provided good support for analysis as well as transparency for innovators. The tool supports a ranking scale from 5 (best) to 1 (worst) and the CS team defined these numbers as follows:

- 5 = very good idea and contains Web 2.0 component (idea is relevant for the "Kiosk of the Future" project)
- 4 = good idea and contains Web 2.0 component (idea is relevant for the "Kiosk of the Future" project)

- 3 = good idea, but does not contain Web 2.0 component (idea is relevant to the Kiosk company but not to the "Kiosk of the Future" project)
- 1 & 2 = "bad idea", i.e. ideas that did not correspond to the published criteria and were not relevant to Valora Retail

The CS team focused on ideas with a ranking of 4 or 5. Ideas with a ranking of 3 were not relevant to the "Kiosk of the Future" project, but they were identified as being potentially valuable for other departments within Valora Retail and were forwarded to them. Since the ranking activity was time-consuming and took several clicks per idea, ideas that were assessed to be 1 or 2 were not ranked at all.

The CS intermediary company had designed the ranking system to be used during the idea submission phase as well as at the end of the project. Since the innovators were motivated by the monetary reward, the CS intermediary company recommended providing rankings during the idea generation process which would result in innovators accordingly adjusting the direction and type of their ideas. The CS team took advantage of this and rated the ideas during the idea generating phase. In addition to providing rankings, the CS team commented on some ideas and highlighted which parts of each idea best matched the goals of Valora Retail. This was done to steer the ideas in the right direction. The CS team initiated no further interaction with the innovators, except for answering specific incoming questions.

In general, the activity level on the platform was much higher than had been expected by Valora Retail and the CS team. One measure of the activity is the number of rankings and comments that took place through the innovators. Ranking by the innovators was very active, as they could earn Atizo "seniority" points with this. Thus, 444 of the 626 ideas were ranked (70.9%). The CS team read all the ideas but only ranked the ones with a 3, 4 or 5 or above, resulting in only 208 ranked ideas (33.2%). And an astonishing 480 ideas (76.7%) had comments by other innovators attached.

During the rating of the ideas many repetitions and ideas building on each were discovered. This presented an unexpected and significant amount of work for the CS team. What made their job a bit easier was that innovators were eager for their idea to win and innovators would watch each other carefully for duplicate ideas and when detected would link from the duplicate idea to their own original idea in the comment field. Interestingly, some innovators developed a repartee, as evidenced in some of the back-and-forth commenting that some ideas provoked. In one instance a innovator enhanced an existing idea which was then commented on and enhanced some more by the innovator of the original idea with both of them agreeing (via the comment field), that they would split any money awarded to either idea. Such internal agreements aside, the official Atizo policy is to award the chronologically first idea of a group of similar ideas, unless a following idea contributes a significant improvement on the original idea, in which case the monetary award would need to be split.

The number of ideas submitted, the duplications and the need for several clicks per rating meant that the CS team had to invest more time than had been planned for this phase. Consequently, a few actions that might have increased the quality of ideas, such as dialogues with the innovators, could not be performed simply due to a lack of time.

Assessment Phase

Upon termination of the virtual idea generation, the CS team carefully analyzed the submitted ideas. Of all the ideas submitted, 60% of the ideas were not considered relevant for Valora Retail and therefore not ranked. From the further 204 ideas (33%), 140 ideas (22%) were estimated to be relevant for Valora Retail, but not relevant for the project "Kiosk of the Future". Therefore, only 64 ideas were assessed as being relevant for the "Kiosk of the Future" project and of those, 19 were rewarded and considered for further analysis and processing (Fig. 2).

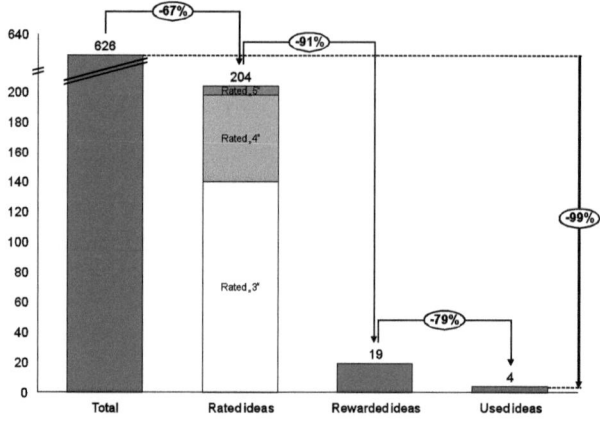

Figure 2: Total number of ideas generated and used

The CS intermediary company gave the moderators two weeks after conclusion of the idea generation phase to sort through the comments and reward the 3000 CHF to the innovators. The CS intermediary company does not prescribe how to distribute the money, but two basic models were considered: dividing the reward evenly, or giving a larger amount to the top ideas. The CS team decided to reward the top two ideas with 400 CHF and equally distribute the remaining reward to gain the innovators' goodwill towards CS and possibly the Kiosk brand.

Following this step the Valora Retail and the CS team were free to use the ideas individually or in any combination, since the innovators seceded their rights to their submitted ideas at the conclusion of the CS process.

Post-processing Phase

After the ranking of ideas, the CS team grouped all 626 ideas by category. Interestingly, the vast majority of ideas could be clustered into just seven topic areas, with a few ideas spanning more than one category (number of ideas in parenthesis): 1) Products and services (222), 2) Public displays and terminals (131), 3) Mobile offerings (75), 4) Intersection of physical store with digital information (74), 5) Pickup services (73), 6) Payment (26) and 7) Games (16). A further 69 ideas were uncategorized and irrelevant to the project. The distribution of the ideas was taken to show a trend and an emphasis of topics and was welcomed by Valora Retail as confirmation that several ongoing projects were on the right track, e.g. a public display test.

These categories were further prioritized and some removed due to existing projects (payment) or lack of internal support (pickup services). Thus, the CS team entered the second phase of idea evaluation and validation with four categories: 1) Displays, 2) Products and services, 3) Intersection of physical store with digital information and 4) Games, both digital and non-digital.

The CS team prepared the 14 top ideas for a selection workshop conducted with an "idea jury" made up of stakeholders from different departments of Valora Retail (Strategic Marketing, Corporate Communications, Kiosk Management, Conception & Construction Management). In preparation, the CS team described each idea in detail and proposed a ranking based on market impact and implementation complexity and gave a recommendation (see Fig. 3). For example, in category 1) Displays, the idea "digital pinboard" (Fig. 3, star "1"), was judged to have a high impact but be easy to implement and was recommended by the CS team for implementation. By contrast, the idea "Tryvertising", where customers could belong to a club that would be given first access to new products, was rated as moderately complex due to logistical considerations (Fig. 3, star "2"). The idea of sending a short message via Twitter for each sale conducted was a favorite in the CS team, but was rated to have a low impact with high implementation complexity (Fig. 3, star "3"). In the games category, a treasure hunt (Geocaching) would be moderately difficult to implement, yet have a high impact (Fig. 3, star "4").

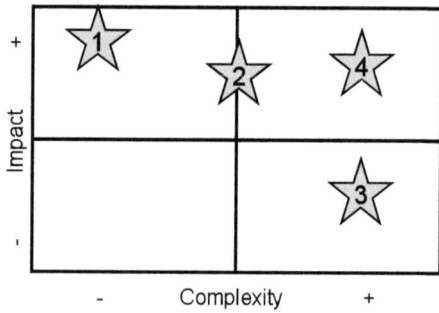

Figure 3: Example of assessment according to complexity and impact of four ideas

These assessments by the CS team were provided to the workshop participants and they were asked to prepare for the workshop by evaluating each idea along a matrix of criteria: customer acceptance, alignment with company vision, alignment with Kiosk strategy, uniqueness and "coolness", implementation complexity, potential impact in the media, ability to multiply idea, revenue potential. These individual evaluations were discussed and gathered during the workshop and produced 4 clear favorite ideas which were selected for implementation.

The "Kiosk of the Future" project very early on determined that there was a need to examine some ideas in a more controlled lab setting and that some ideas needed to be implemented in an actual Kiosk to be understood. Thus, a small number of the top ideas from the CS process (ranked 4 or 5) were seen as interesting ideas, but impossible to execute due to technological, logistical or business constraints and were put aside to be tested in a lab setting.

The 4 top ideas were combined with other ideas originating from internal Valora Retail teams which had been working on the project or generated during internal workshops including external experts. From those three sources, a total of 7 ideas are today in implementation in the "Kiosk of the Future" of which 4 were generated through the CS process.

Discussion

This case study demonstrated how successful the CS approach can be as part of an Open Innovation process by bringing in ideas that would not have been able to come from within the company due to internal barriers. A few lessons learned along the way are summarized here.

Expert knowledge in the CS team

Expert knowledge is needed in the team for the deliberation and preparation phases, as well as the assessment and post-processing. In the early phases, a careful preparation helps ensure a successful outcome of the effort. In the assessment of the ideas, a strong domain knowledge and knowledge of the business proved valuable in gaining the most from both the ideas that were central to the project but also in order to know which ideas might be usefully passed on to interested departments. Finally, the post-processing and implementation requires a deep understanding of the business processes involved.

Question Formulation

The quality of ideas generated in a CS process rests to a large degree on the careful and precise wording of the question posed to the innovators. Drafts of the question were sent out for review and refined iteratively until the majority of reviewers had the same understanding from the written question as the CS team was hoping to transmit.

In formulating the question (and later in assessing the ideas generated) a certain technological bias of the innovator population must be assumed since a fairly high level of computer literacy as well as an affinity for technology is required to be involved in a CS platform at this point in time.

Budgeting time and effort

Monitoring the ideas during the active idea generation phase and the guiding of the innovators through ongoing ranking and commenting took a much larger amount of time than expected.

It is worth noting that while most innovators aimed to have original ideas so that they would be the chronological first one to post the idea and thus reap the reward, the ideas were still remarkably similar and hard to distinguish from each other if looked at from an implementation or business perspective (i.e. while two ideas might look different in their wording, in a real-world implementation they would just be two features in one program). The similarity of the ideas made for quite repetitive reading for the CS team. However, this did allow a clear categorization of the ideas into only four categories and within those, a clear identification of the favorite topics (public displays and the intersection of the physical store with digital information).

The final number of ideas generated during the CS process described in this case study was higher than expected and consequently required a much larger effort to categorize and rank than had been budgeted. Thus the assessment phase was longer in duration than had been planned. If more time had been available, a productive use would have been to initiate a dialogue with innovators providing the top ideas. More time should have been allocated in the resource planning phase. Best practices indicate that an increase in workload should be planned at the outset of the project and during the first 4 weeks where the bulk of the ideas are generated (Muhdi et al 2010).

The public nature of CS

A clear difference in focus exists between the phases of idea generation and assessment one the one hand and post-processing on the other. On a CS platform that is open to the public, both idea generation and assessment are therefore visible to the public. As such, the conduct of the company needs to be aligned with corporate policy, as well as communication strategies. The involvement of the communication department is particularly important since the ideas are visible to the press and might be re-printed; which happened during the project described in this paper (Vogel 2010). The process of selecting and rewarding the top ideas needs to be understood by the public. This might lead, for example, to rewarding a great idea, even if it is clear to the CS team that the idea cannot be implemented due to company-internal constraints or strategies.

Post-processing and implementation

As public as the idea generation and assessment phases are, the opposite is true of the post-processing phase. Here the best ideas from the CS process become just one of the inputs into a larger discussion of what ideas to implement and how. In this stage, ideas might be joined into a larger idea or mixed with concepts developed independently of the CS process. At this point, cross-department workshops are advisable in which people with diverse viewpoints assess the business-aspects of implementing the ideas.

Regardless of the publicly awarded "best" ideas from the CS process, the decision of whether and how they fit into the business is solely in the domain of the company. Thus In the presented case, of the 626 ideas generated, 64 ideas were relevant for the project and while 19 were awarded, in the end 4 were taken into the next steps of implementation. While this number is small, the ideas not used are still useful in providing weight to the ideas chosen, e.g. the large number of ideas in the top two categories (public displays and the customer interest in the intersection between the physical store and digital information), gave weight to the ideas chosen that represented those categories.

LIMITATIONS AND FUTURE RESEARCH

This case study is focused on a Swiss company operating in a Swiss market. Also, the CS intermediary used is Swiss, increasing the risk of the observations being not general enough. Similarly, only one industry – retail – is examined. However, the experiences described and lessons learned are compatible with those found in international literature. Further research could compare similar cases in other industries and countries.

CONCLUSIONS

This paper described a CS process in which Valora Retail generated 626 ideas over the space of 7 weeks by hiring a CS intermediary. Having access to an existing community of innovators allowed for a quick start of the project, which produced 19 top ideas that were selected and awarded during the assessment phase. These ideas were refined in the post-processing phase. This was a successful CS project for Valora Retail resulting in 4 ideas that are ready for implementation in the „Kiosk of the Future".

REFERENCES

1. Altshuller, G. (1996) And suddenly the inventor appeared: Triz, the theory of inventive problem solving, Technical Innovation Center, Worcester, Massachusetts.
2. Atizo (2010) Community Insights, http://blog.atizo.com/2010/06/. Accessed January 2011.
3. Chesbrough, HW. (2003) Open innovation: the new imperative for creating and profiting from technology. Harvard Business Press
4. Diehl, M., and Stroebe, W. (1987) Productivity loss in brainstorming groups - towards the solution of a riddle. Journal of Personality and Social Psychology, 53, 497-509.
5. Ebner, W., Leimeister, JM., et al. (2009) Community engineering for innovation: the ideas competition as a method to nurture a virtual community for innovation. R&D Management, 39, 342-356.
6. ENKEL, E. and Gassmann, O., et al. (2009) Open R&D and open innovation; exploring the phenomena. R&D Management, 39, 311-316.
7. Fichter, K. (2009) Innovation communities; the role of networks in Open Innovation. R&D Management, 39, 357-371.
8. Galli H. (2010) Die Ideensammler. Tagesanzeiger, Zürich, Switzerland, 9.2.2010
9. Howe J. (2006) The rise of crowdsourcing. Wired magazine, Issue 14.06.
10. Howe J. (2008) Crowdsourcing : how the power of the crowd is driving the future of business, Random House Business, London.
11. L. Muhdi, M. Daiber, S. Friesike, R. Boutellier (2010) Crowdsourcing: an alternative idea generation approach in the early innovation process, Proceedings of the XXI ISPIM Conference on "The Dynamics of Innovation", Bilbao, Spain, June 6-9, 2010. ISBN 978-952-214-926.
12. Piller, FT. and Walcher, D. (2006) Toolkits for idea competitions. a novel method to integrate users in new product development. R&D Management, 307-318.
13. Vogel B. (2010) Twittern am Kiosk. SonntagsZeitung, Zürich, Switzerland, 22.08.2010.

8.2.3. Motivational factors affecting participation and contribution of members in two different Swiss innovation communities

Motivational factors affecting participation and contribution of members in two different Swiss innovation communities

Abstract: Different types of virtual innovation-related communities have emerged in recent years. These are increasingly being utilized by companies from different industries as a tool to efficiently source knowledge from diverse groups of individuals and thus to nourish internal innovations. Based on a case study research methodology this study investigated the impact 39 motivational factors have on the participation and contribution of members of two different innovation communities, i.e. an online Swiss innovation intermediary community (n=48) and the off-line internal innovation community of a Swiss bank (n=69). Results showed many similarities yet 16 significant differences between the perception of members of the two investigated innovation communities. Results showed that reward related items (monetary and non-monetary) are top motivators for the intermediary community only. Items such as 'Webcam option', 'Chat function', 'Connection with other social network platforms', were perceived as low motivators by both communities. Derived from the findings, we discuss how the nature of the innovation community has an influence on the motivation and measures potentially leading to higher participation and contribution efficiency.

Keywords: Open Innovation; Crowdsourcing; Virtual innovation communities; Motivational factors; Switzerland.

1 Introduction

The Open Innovation phenomena, observed and described by Chesbrough in 2006, depicts the increase in openness of organizations towards their environment and the utilization of targeted inflows and outflows of knowledge in order to accelerate internal innovation, and expand the markets for external use of innovation, respectively (Chesbrough, 2006). Different Open Innovation approaches and practices have been discussed in an ever growing body of literature, by academics and practitioners alike (Chesbrough, 2003a, Chesbrough, 2003b, Enkel et al., 2009, Gassmann, 2006, Huston, 2006). Within this context, it is today widely acknowledged that users and user networks are an important source of innovation. They have been identified to be the major drivers of many innovations in different industries (Lettl et al., 2006). Hence, an ever-growing number of companies strive to develop appropriate approaches or implement internal processes that enable a systematic exploitation of the knowledge and skills of users as well as other stakeholders to nourish internal innovation process. With the purpose to actively harness the new wave of innovation and creativity, different approaches were developed and described in scientific and practitioner literature. In the late 1980's, user-centric approaches such as the participatory design (Ehn and Kyng, 1987) and the lead-user approach (von Hippel, 1988, von Hippel, 2006) were largely discussed. Presently and due to the significant developments of the Internet, novel information and communication technologies (ICTs) and the social media, companies have been provided with new means and tools to harness external knowledge (Fichter, 2009, Gordon, 2008, Ebner et al., 2009). In this context, particularly the developments of virtual communities and virtual innovation communities have opened up a wide range of novel possibilities for companies to gather external information that has the potential to support and improve e.g. internal R&D, marketing and communication. In the past years, different types of virtual innovation communities have emerged. Some are firm-hosted and are online, e.g. in form of an online ideas platform such as Dells 'ideaStorm.com' while others are operated offline within a company setting, e.g. in the form of an internal innovation community, as done at Bombardier Aerospace. Other virtual innovation communities are fostered by innovation intermediaries or virtual knowledge brokers. These are actors who leverage the Internet to support third parties' innovation activities by, for example, enabling companies to purposively collect external knowledge. They mostly operate autonomously and maintain online communities consisting of various groups of individuals, including specialists from different scientific fields like InnoCentive, or a heterogeneous group of individuals with diverse and different backgrounds and interests like Atizo. Intermediaries enable companies to save cost and resources, extend their reach to diverse knowledge (Bishop, 2009) and allow them to have a richer dialogue with target groups of individuals mainly because of their perceived neutrality (Verona and Prandelli, 2006). Innovation intermediaries have attracted many clients and have influenced and modified the conventional innovation processes of many companies from different industries (Lakhani, 2009, Pisanno, 2008). One study has shown that up to 30 % of internal problems that could not be solved internally had a successful outcome with the help of intermediaries (Lakhani et al., 2006).

Virtual innovation communities (online or offline) have till date been utilized by companies from different industries as an instrument to source knowledge from masses of individuals (crowds) independent of their geographical location. This Internet-enabled approach, today known as Crowdsourcing (Howe, 2006), has gained increasing popularity in recent years (Muhdi et al., 2010). Crowdsourcing is defined as the outsourcing of a task (e.g. the idea generation), which usually is performed by an employee or a contractor to a large group of people or a community (a crowd) through a virtual open call. Today, Crowdsourcing is commonly utilized for idea generation in the early innovation phase (Bonabeau, 2009, Ebner et al., 2009, Muhdi et al., 2010), a phase that has been identified in literature to be decisive for success in product innovations (Dwyer, 1991, Verworn, 2009). Thus, in order to achieve the best outcome, the main challenge of companies, looking to successfully utilize Crowdsourcing nowadays, often lies in understanding, choosing and motivating the appropriate innovation community.

This paper aims to explore and enhance the understanding of the varying importance of motivational factors to participate and collaborate in two types of innovation communities, i.e. internal innovation communities and the communities of innovation intermediaries. Since the contribution in existing innovation communities is voluntary, and because it is generally challenging to motivate people to freely share their time and knowledge, we believe it is essential to know and understand motivational factors in order to optimize internal strategies for attracting qualified contributors and retaining existing participants for a long time. Furthermore, in order to enhance and increase innovation-related community-generated content, various measures for effective participation and collaboration are suggested and discussed.

2 Literature review

User-driven or user-centred innovation is a research field that has found great interest amongst academics and practitioners alike. Different approaches were developed in this context, starting with participatory design (PD) which has its origin in the pioneering work of Kirsten Nygaard in the 1970's (Ehn and Kyng, 1987, Schuler and Namioka, 1993). Participatory design became a label for design and development processes in which end-users were invited to participate and contribute, not simply as critics and evaluators of product and system concepts, but as co-designers (Buur and Matthews, 2008). PD is an approach where stakeholders are engaged in co-design activities throughout the innovation process (Ehn and Kyng, 1987, Buur and Bagger, 1999, Holmquist,

2004) which is typically applied in the early stages of the product design (Pals et al., 2008).

In the late 1980's, Eric von Hippel documented that the users, rather than the manufacturers, are often the source of innovation (von Hippel, 1988). The lead-user approach was developed (von Hippel, 1988, von Hippel, 2006) and was based on the assumption that certain types of users experience market needs months or years ahead of the bulk of the market. Some of these users are in a position to benefit greatly from and especially by products that meet these needs. Furthermore, some of these users also possess skills and necessary tools to modify, re-design, adapt, etc. the existing product or services to meet these needs. These groups of people were named "lead users" by Eric von Hippel and were described to be more reliable predictors of the future market compared to traditional market research.

Unlike other user-centric approaches such as the empathic design approach (Leonard and Rayport, 1997), where a small team of researchers, such as an engineer, a human-factors expert and a designer, observe people in their normal home or work environment in order to see how they utilize and interact with the products under study, the main objectives of the two mentioned user-centric innovation approaches are to establish environments that enhance active interaction between e.g. the designer and the user(s) and make mutual learning possible. This way the users' perspective can be incorporated in research and design (Rohracher, 2005) and the articulation of the user's needs can be enabled through various efforts.

Today modern ICTs and social media technologies provide companies with additional tools that facilitate the attempt to reach appropriate users or stakeholders that are in possession of valuable knowledge or skills which can be used to push internal innovation. However, reaching these individuals is not enough, it is important to understand how to motivate these appropriate individuals to voluntarily contribute, and thus create value for the companies.

An increasing amount of current literature addresses the importance of revealing motivational factors leading to people's participation and collaboration in virtual innovation communities as well as factors that lead to maximising their input. Knowing and understanding these factors can have a significant impact on the success of the application of innovation communities in nourishing company innovations. Research conducted in the fields of collective creativity and online communities has revealed general motivational factors guiding people and causing them to visit, join and actively contribute in online communities. Amongst others, motivational factors such as fun (Nov, 2007, Antikainen, 2008), monetary rewards (Antikainen and Väätäjä, 2010) firm and peer recognition (Antikainen and Väätäjä, 2010, Jeppesen, 2006, Lerner and Tirole, 2002), reciprocity (Wasko and Faraj, 2000) and sharing an experience and enhancement of professional reputation (McLure Wasko and Faraj, 2000) have been identified to be important. Furthermore, it has been suggested that the nature and the purpose of an online community also has an effect on the motivations of community members (McLure Wasko and Faraj, 2000, Wasko and Faraj, 2000, Franke and Shah, 2003). In the context of Open Innovation, studies have been performed around the motivation of free sharing of information in innovation communities (Franke and Shah, 2003, Jeppesen, 2006). The motivation of individuals to contribute in online open source software projects (von Krogh and von Hippel, 2006, von Hippel and Von Krogh, 2006) without a secure reward has also been described. Here, reputation, recognition among peers and the need for improved products were shown to be important motivational factors. Additionally, participants' motivations (external and internal factors) were found to be drivers of initial and continued engagement, effort and contributions (Hars and Ou, 2002, Hertel et al., 2003, Roberts et al., 2006, Shah, 2006). In more recent articles the effect of rewarding strategies on the motivation to participate in innovation communities of intermediaries was investigated (Antikainen and Väätäjä, 2010). Moreover, some motivational factors influencing collaboration in Open Innovation communities were observed and discussed (Antikainen and Ahonen, 2010). Antikaianen and Ahornen claimed that monetary rewards alone are not sufficient to motivate contributors of innovation communities to collaborate. They found intangible factors such as community cooperation, learning and entertainment to be important in this context.

Given that the nature of innovation communities has an impact on the outcome of initiated Crowdsourcing projects, it is essential to know which factors contribute to participants' motivation in different types of communities. Companies aiming to recruit and retain volunteering contributors should focus their marketing, recruitment, and retention efforts on the motivational factors which have the highest relative importance for the targeted innovation community.

While the insights in available literature of motivational research concentrates on revealing selected motivational factors for either intermediaries, innovation communities, firm-hosted user communities, or OSS communities, there is to our knowledge no research to date that has directly compared motivations for different types of innovation communities.

3 Research design

In this paper, we applied an empirical case study research design (Eisenhardt, 1989, Yin, 2003, Stake, 1995) in order to obtain deeper insights into factors affecting the contributors' motivation to participate in two different types of innovation communities, i.e. internal innovation community and an intermediary innovation community. Subsequently a quantitative data analysis was performed.

3.1. Case studies

Data sets were collected from the internal innovation community of PostFinance and the intermediary innovation community of Atizo. PostFinance is a Swiss bank and an employer of around 3'000 people. In 2010, PostFinance initiated the internal innovation community as a pilot project to test the Crowdsourcing approach for internal idea generation. Atizo is a prominent Swiss Open Innovation intermediary which operates a community consisting of around 8'000 members (2010) with heterogeneous interests and backgrounds.

3.2. Data sources and project details

Following a thorough literature research and an internal deliberation, an e-survey was designed to include 39 motivational factors. The e-surveys were sent to members of the two studied innovation communities. All of the items in the e-survey were presented as statements to which contributors were asked to state their personal perceived importance on a five-point Likert scale of 1 to 5 (1= "Unimportant", 2= "Partially unimportant", 3. "Neutral", 4. "Important", 5. "Very important"). A brief description of our study and the link to the e-survey was sent to 121 community members and employees of PostFinance. These all had been chosen internally from different departments to participate in the pilot project and each had at least submitted one idea during a previous idea generation project. Simultaneously, a brief description of our study and the link to the e-survey was integrated in Atizos monthly community e-newsletter and additionally posted on Atizos Facebook, Twitter, and Blog page. The two independent e-surveys were performed in August 2010 and returned within three or two weeks, respectively. 69 PostFinance employees and 48 Atizo community members completed the e-survey. The e-surveys were performed using the online tool Unipark and the results were analyzed with the PASW (SPSS) statistics software.

In this paper we applied an empirical case study research design (Eisenhardt, 1989, Stake, 1995, Yin, 2003) in order to obtain deeper insight on factors affecting the contributors' motivation to participate in two different types of innovation communities, i.e. internal innovation community and intermediary innovation community. Subsequently a quantitative data analysis was performed.

4 Findings

The e-surveys of this study, which were performed with two different virtual innovation communities, i.e. the community of the innovation intermediary Atizo and the internal innovation community of the Swiss bank PostFinance, have granted insights which increase the overall understanding of important factors contributing to the motivation of community members to participate and add content within innovation related virtual communities. In addition, the extracted data has allowed us to formulate suggestions for strategic measures aimed at increasing participation and contribution efficiency.

Results from the two innovation communities showed similarities as well as differences in the perceived importance of different motivational items for participation and contribution. In order to demonstrate the differences at a glance, the mean values of each item for the two communities were calculated and plotted Figure 1. The mean values are illustrated with a 95% confidence interval (CI).

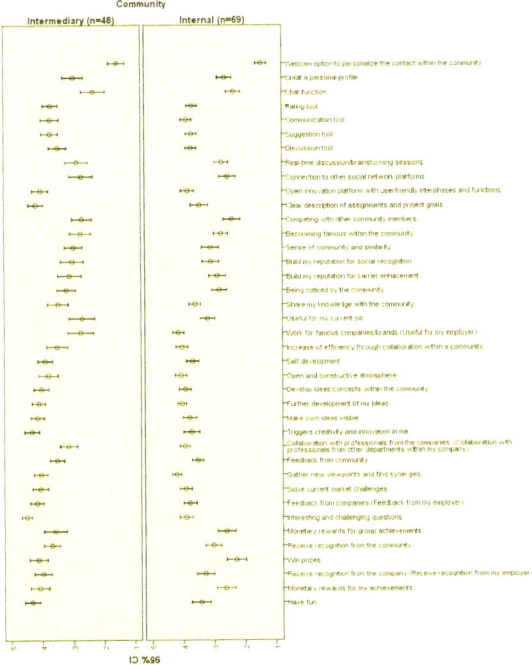

Figure 1 Plot of the mean value of all motivational factors for the two investigated innovation communities. Intermediary (n=48) vs. internal innovation community (n=69). Formulations of the items for the internal innovation community that differ from the intermediary community are in brackets.

Table 1 illustrates the mean values of all motivational factors for the two innovation communities. The motivational factors are arranged according to their mean values (highest starting from up).

Motivation factor (Intermediary innovation community)	Mean
Interesting and challenging questions	4.50
Have fun	4.33
Triggers creativity and innovation in me	4.33
Clear description of assignments and project goals	4.19
Feedback from companies (Employer)	4.17
Make own ideas visible	4.15
Win prizes	4.13
Develop further on my ideas	4.10
Monetary rewards for my achievements	4.08
Solve current market challenges	4.06
Gather new viewpoints and find synergies	4.04
Open innovation platform with userfriendly interphases and functions	4.04
Develop ideas/concepts within the community	4.02
Receive recognition from the company (my employer)	3.98
Self development	3.90
Open and constructive atmosphere	3.79
Suggestion tool	3.73
Communication tool	3.73
Rating tool	3.71
Receive recognition from the community	3.69
Monetary rewards for group achievements	3.58
Feedback from community	3.52
Increase of efficiency through collaboration within a community	3.50
Discussion tool	3.48
Share my knowledge with the community	3.48
Being noticed by the community	3.21
Collaboration with professionals from the companies (other departments within my company)	3.15
Build my reputation for carrier enhancement	3.10
Build my reputation for social recognition	3.02
Sense of community and similarity	2.98
Creat a personal profile	2.98
Realtime discussion/brainstorming sessions	2.88
Work for famous companies/brands	2.75
Becoming famous within the community	2.75
Connection to other social network platforms	2.73
Useful for my current job	2.71
Competing with other community members	2.71
Chat function	2.33
Webcam option to personalize the contact within the community	1.56

Motivation factor (Internal innovation community)	Mean
Gather new viewpoints and find synergies	4.20
Work for famous companies/brands	4.14
Open and constructive atmosphere	4.06
Develop further on my ideas	4.03
Increase of efficiency through collaboration within a community	4.03
Collaboration with professionals from the companies (other departments within my company)	3.94
Develop ideas/concepts within the community	3.93
Solve current market challenges	3.91
Interesting and challenging questions	3.90
Communication tool	3.87
Open innovation platform with userfriendly interphases and functions	3.84
Make own ideas visible	3.78
Feedback from companies (Employer)	3.78
Triggers creativity and innovation in me	3.72
Discussion tool	3.72
Suggestion tool	3.71
Rating tool	3.70
Self development	3.68
Share my knowledge with the community	3.61
Feedback from community	3.52
Clear description of assignments and project goals	3.46
Have fun	3.43
Receive recognition from the company (my employer)	3.29
Useful for my current job	3.20
Sense of community and similarity	3.12
Build my reputation for social recognition	3.10
Receive recognition from the community	3.03
Build my reputation for carrier enhancement	2.88
Being noticed by the community	2.83
Becoming famous within the community	2.77
Realtime discussion/brainstorming sessions	2.74
Creat a personal profile	2.64
Monetary rewards for my achievements	2.62
Monetary rewards for group achievements	2.61
Connection to other social network platforms	2.55
Competing with other community members	2.41
Chat function	2.35
Win prizes	2.29
Webcam option to personalize the contact within the community	1.45

Table 1 Ranking of the mean value of all motivational factors for the two investigated innovation communities. Left: intermediary innovation community, right: internal innovation community.

An independent t-test was performed to detect whether the observed differences of the perceived importance of the motivational factors between the two communities show any statistical significance ($p \leq 0.05$). Results showed that 16 out of the 39 investigated motivational factors differ significantly between the two communities (Table 2).

Motivation factor	t-test Sig. (2-tailed)
Work for famous companies/brands	0.000
Collaboration with professionals from the companies (other departments within my company)	0.000
Interesting and challenging questions	0.000
Triggers creativity and innovation in me	0.000
Clear description of assignments and project goals	0.000
Have fun	0.000
Monetary rewards for my achievements	0.000
Monetary rewards for group achievements	0.000
Win prizes	0.000
Make own ideas visible	0.001
Receive recognition from the company (my employer)	0.001
Receive recognition from the community	0.001
Increase of efficiency through collaboration within a community	0.008
Feedback from companies (employer)	0.015
Useful for my current job	0.039
Being noticed by the community	0.047

Table 2 16 out of 39 motivational factors showing significant difference in the t-test ($p \leq 0.05$) between the two innovation communities.

In order to simplify the interpretation of the findings, related items of the e-surveys were aggregated and the following six categories: 1) Social aspect, 2) Competition, 3) Learning, 4) Sense of efficiency, 5) Rewards and 6) Platform features (Figure 2). The choice of these categories was made according to two criteria: a) to form as few categories as possible, b) integrate categories found in literature. Some items had the potential of fitting to more than one motivational category; however, following an internal discussion the estimated most appropriate category was chosen. Figure 2 illustrates the investigated 39 motivational items categorized into six categories.

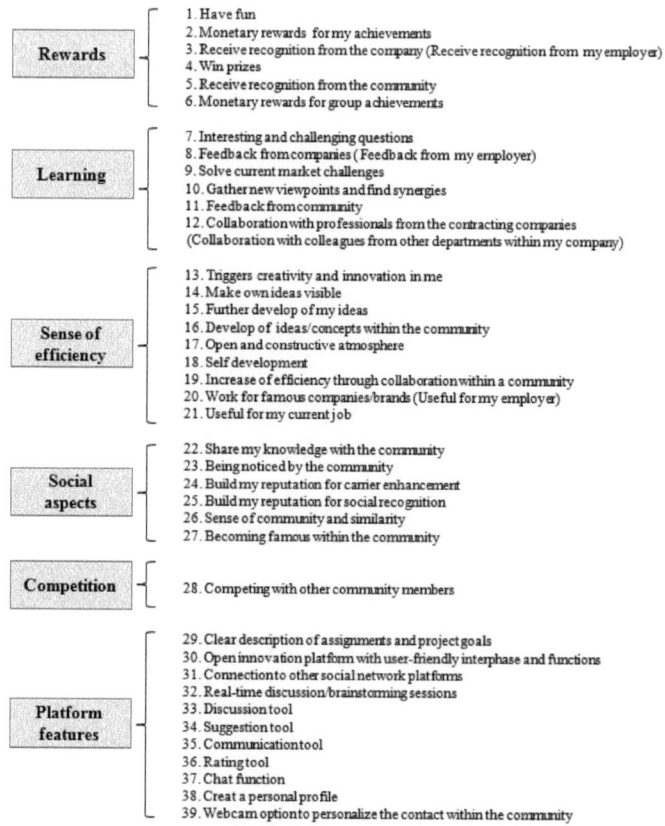

Figure 2 Investigated motivational factors categorized into six categories. Formulations of the items for the internal innovation community that differ from the intermediary community are in brackets.

To support the detection of potential trends and to facilitate data interpretation, a simple depiction of the achieved data was performed aiming to illustrate the ranking of the six categories for the two innovation communities (Table 3). The rankings are based on the average of the mean values of the items within each category where the items were given equal weight. The intermediary community ranking of the categories showed the following order (1=highest - 6=lowest): 1. Rewards, 2. Learning, 3. Sense of efficiency, 4. Platform features, 5. Social aspect and 6. Competition. The ranking of the categories according to the internal community was as follows: 1. Learning, 2. Sense of efficiency, 3. Platform features, 4. Social aspect, 5. Rewards and 6. Competition (Table 3).

Category ranking	Intermediary community (mean value)	Internal community (mean value)
1	Rewards (3.97)	Learning (3.88)
2	Learning (3.91)	Sense of efficiency (3.84)
3	Sense of efficiency (3.69)	Platform features (3.09)
4	Platform features (3.21)	Social aspects (3.05)
5	Social aspects (3.09)	Rewards (2.88)
6	Competition (2.71)	Competition (2.41)

Table 3 Ranking of the categories: intermediary vs. internal innovation community

4.1. Top motivators of the intermediary innovation community members

In this paper we define top motivators as those items that showed a mean value higher than 4.0 based on the five-point Likert scale used. In the following sections we will elaborate on the nature of top motivators within the two communities. Additionally, we indicate the percentage (in brackets) of community members that rated the items in our e-surveys to be 'important', or 'very important'.

Members of the intermediary community are, as illustrated above, highly motivated by factors belonging to the category 'Rewards'. Notably the non-monetary item 'Have fun' (85.4%) and the monetary items 'Win prizes' (79.2%) and 'Monetary rewards for my achievements' (75.1%) were identified as top motivators for the participation and contribution of these community members.

Furthermore, four out of six items belonging to the category 'Learning' were identified as top motivators of the intermediary community and were as follows: 'Interesting and challenging questions' (97.9%) 'Feedback from companies' (79.2%), 'Solve current market challenges' (85.5%), 'Gather new viewpoints and find synergies' (81.3%). From the category 'Sense of efficiency', the following items were amongst the top ranked: 'Triggers my creativity and innovation' (89.6%), 'Make my own ideas visible' (87.6%), 'Further development on my ideas' (81.3%), 'Develop ideas/concepts within the community' (79.2%).

4.2. Top motivators of the internal innovation community members

The majority of the items rated by the internal innovation community had a mean value between 3.0 and 4.0. For that reason, only a few items were here identified as top motivators (a mean value higher than 4.0).

The highest rated item was found to be 'Gather new viewpoints and find synergies' (89.8 %) which belongs to the category 'Learning'. The remaining four top motivational items of this community belong to the category 'Sense of efficiency' and are the following: 'Work for a famous company' (85.5 %), 'Open and constructive atmosphere' (81.1%), 'Further development on my ideas' (85.5%), and 'Increase of efficiency through collaboration within a community' (81.2 %).

4.3. Low motivators of both innovation communities

The definition of 'the lower end' in this study is when an item shows a mean value lower than 3.0. In the following the percentage in brackets illustrates the share of individuals (Intermediary community vs. internal community) who have rated the items 'partially unimportant' or 'unimportant'. Five items belonging to the category 'Platform features' appeared in the lower end of the ranking lists of both communities and were the following: 'Webcam option to personalize the contact within the community' (83.4% vs. 85.5%),

'Chat function' (54.5% vs. 52.2%), 'Connection with other social network platforms' (52.1% vs. 39.1%), 'Real-time discussions/brainstorming sessions' (33.3% vs. 33.3%) and 'Create personal profile' (29.2% vs. 37.6%). Specifically for the intermediary community the following items were in the lower end of the ranking list: 'Useful for my current job' (47.9%), 'Work for famous companies/brands' (37.6%), 'Sense of community and similarity' (20.8%). The internal community views winning prizes (55%), monetary incentives for the individual (40.6%) and group achievements (40.5%) as low motivators. This reflects once more the low rating of the item category "Rewards" (see Table 3).

4.4. Motivation factors with largest differences between the two communities

Large difference in ranking between the two communities was observed in the following items: 'Win prizes', 'Monetary rewards for my achievements', 'Work for famous companies/brands'*, 'Monetary rewards for group achievements', 'Have fun', 'Collaboration with professionals from the companies (other departments within my company)', 'Clear description of assignments and project goals', 'Receive recognition from the company (my employer)', 'Receive recognition from the community', 'Triggers creativity and innovation in me', 'Interesting and challenging questions', 'Increase of efficiency through collaboration within a community'* and 'Useful for my current job'. A large number of these items belong to the category 'Rewards' and 'Sense of efficiency'. The items with * were ranked higher by the internal community.

5 Discussion

This paper aims at highlighting the varying importance of motivational factors to participate and collaborate in two types of innovation communities, i.e. an innovation intermediary community and an internal innovation community. Since the nature of the two communities differ, the contribution in these innovation communities is voluntarily and it is challenging to motivate people to freely share their time and knowledge, we believe it is essential to know and understand these factors in order to optimize internal strategies to attract qualified contributors and keep existing ones active on a long term basis. Furthermore, in order to enhance and increase innovation-related community-generated content, various measures for effective participation and collaboration are suggested and discussed.

This study has shown that there is a significant difference between the perceived importance of rewards for participation and contribution between the intermediary innovation community and the company-hosted internal innovation community. In coherence with the findings of a previous paper (Antikainen and Väätäjä, 2010), our findings indicate that members who voluntarily contribute in the community find monetary rewards as well as non-monetary rewards to be an important return for their individual contribution. A combination of monetary and non-monetary rewards is thus best used to motivate intermediary community members to participate and contribute. Furthermore, and based on the findings showing that 'Have fun' is a top motivator for the intermediary community, we suggest that intermediaries try to augment this sensation in their members by further investigating into measures that have the potential to positively stimulate the feeling of enjoyment, amusement or pleasure. Members of the internal community, however, did not find any items belonging to the category 'Rewards' highly important for their motivation to participate and contribute within the innovation community (see 4.3). A possible explanation for this finding may be that in a company setting, the participation in an innovation community with the aim to advance the company as a whole is viewed as a liability and less as an additional task beside one's own job.

In general, the importance of the perceived learning aspects with regard to participating and contributing within an innovation community was rather high for both innovation communities. Top motivators were found in the category 'Learning' and suggest that the intermediary community finds it important to be informed about and work on actual business challenges. This finding is in accordance with previous findings within the context of online communities in general (Wasko and Faraj, 2000) that indicate that people participate in online communities in order to keep themselves updated about current ideas and innovations. As a measure to increase contribution we suggest that interested members are regularly informed about active projects e.g. by e-mail, on a community blog or via an e-newsletter. This simple measure can support keeping community members up to date with current projects and encourage them to be active. Furthermore, intermediary community members welcome feedbacks from professionals from the contracting companies – a possible sign that they want to feel that their contribution is noticed and valued. As feedback is often used for the improvement and development of individual skills it is important to encourage contracting companies to distribute constructive feedbacks to the participants' which are active in ongoing company projects. Distributing feedback regularly will potentially increasing members' motivation to take part in further projects. Members of the internal community on the other hand attach great importance on the educational effect of the innovation community. They find it important that the community aids in broadening their own horizon and can possibly be used to identify colleagues in possession of similar ideas and thoughts. The emergence of possible collaborations showed to be important for the community members of the internal community. As Wasko and faraj wrote: "People also find that multiple minds are better than one, making access to a community important for innovation" (Wasko and Faraj, 2000). Building on these findings we suggest internal communities to organize their platform in such a way that ideas are matched with the names or to identify the idea owners. Moreover, simple ways to contact idea owners should be made available.

Numerous items belonging to the category 'Sense of efficiency' appeared as top motivators for both communities. Members of the intermediary community find the community important as a source of inspiration. They found it highly important to be able to virtually bring their own ideas to life and to further develop these ideas individually and in collaboration with other community members. The internal community members however, perceived the usefulness of their participation and contribution for their employer as very important. Furthermore, they clearly state that they value the openness of the platform together with the opportunity they are given to add own ideas and to further develop them in collaboration with other internals. These results speak for an internal innovation community in general. In this context it showed to be appreciated that the system is kept transparent and welcoming towards any suggestion regardless of the internal hierarchy (if any) or the employees positioning in the company.

Surprisingly, many items which appeared on the lowest end of the items rankings of the two innovation communities were identical. These items belong to the categories 'Platform features', 'Competition' and one to the 'Social aspects' and were the following: 'Webcam option', 'Competition with other community members', 'Chat function', 'Connection to other social networking platforms', 'Becoming famous within the community', 'Create a personal profile', 'Real-time discussions/brainstorming sessions'. In accordance with the study from Wasko and Faraj (Wasko and Faraj, 2000) the results of our study indicate that members of both communities do not wish to use / use the platform to socialize, nor to develop personal relationships. Since the members of the investigated communities most probably are members of social networking platforms such as MySpace, Facebook, Xing, etc., and use free online tools, such as Skype, there does not seem to be a desire for an innovation platform offering similar features. Reducing functionalities down to only the necessary, and keeping the platform user-friendly seems to be the rule. Furthermore, the issue of anonymity especially for the intermediary community may be the central important point in this context. Often virtual platforms are preferred due to the fact that they help people express their thoughts more openly in comparison with, for example, physical workshops where the face-to-face reaction of others can be intimidating.

Interestingly, the competition factor turned out to be an unimportant motivator to participate and contribute in both of the two Swiss innovation communities.

To a certain extent, this research confirms as previously suggested in literature (McLure Wasko and Faraj, 2000, Wasko and Faraj, 2000, Franke and Shah, 2003) that the nature and the purpose of an online community has an effect on the motivation of community members. Our findings indicate that the top motivators of the intermediary community such as 'Interesting and challenging questions' and 'Have fun' (Table 1) are rather related to personal interests of the members. People contribute to achieve incentives, have fun, learn and be informed about ongoing market challenges. The intermediary innovation platform is available to anyone who is interested in innovation. The contribution there is completely voluntarily and seems to be conducted similar to a hobby. However, in the setting of the internal innovation platform, the company is the initiator and the employees are the contributors. This setting, according to our findings, affects the motivation pattern of the members. Here top motivators such as 'gather new viewpoints and find synergies' and 'work for a famous company' (Table 1) are rather related to professional interests. Findings indicate that the members of the internal innovation community members welcome such a platform because it gives them the freedom to express themselves (in form of answers to internal challenges or ideas) in environment free of (or with minimized) hierarchies. Yet, the platform is perceived as a company provided working tool which aids finding internal synergies and initiate collaborations with similar minded colleagues across the organization.

6 Conclusion

6.1. Contribution

Our study makes several important contributions to current literature. First, our results increase the understanding of motivational factors affecting the participation and contribution of members in innovation related communities. Second, it highlights the similarities and differences in perceived importance of different motivational factors between two different innovation communities, i.e. a Swiss innovation intermediary community and an internal innovation community of a Swiss bank. Understanding the nature of the innovation community and the motivational factors affecting contribution and active involvement in innovation communities is significant for the increasing of project success. Although some studies have examined similar aspects of motivation or participation, a large number has concentrated solely on one type of community e.g. OSS communities. To our knowledge, no study so far has simultaneously investigated two different types of innovation communities. It is essential to consider the motivational system in order to understand how successful an innovation community attracts and sustains participants. Third, we have formulated suggestions for practitioners for measurements to increase participation and contribution efficiency in intermediary and internal innovation communities.

Like many studies based on survey design, this study may potentially suffer from a response bias. For example, enthusiastic contributors were more likely to participate in our e-survey than less active contributors. Furthermore thus not at all motivated to join an innovation community were not asked.

6.2. Practical implications

Our findings have practical implications for managing innovation-related online communities. This study highlights the difference between an intermediary innovation community and an internal innovation community and supports, to a certain extent, companies in their choice whether to create internal communities or to consider an innovation intermediary. Moreover, by highlighting motivational factors important for participation and contribution, the insights of this study can be of aid for companies aiming to create more motivating environments for collective innovation processes.

6.3. Further research

While the findings of this study are based on e-surveys conducted with existing community members, it is important to know the motivations of non-community members as well. Furthermore, the link between the motivation and the quality of the submissions and important factors motivating 'appropriate' contributors is likely to be of interest to innovation researchers and managers.

References and Notes

ANTIKAINEN, M. & AHONEN, M. (2010) Motivating and supporting collaboration in open innovation. European Journal of Innovation Management, 13, 100-119.

ANTIKAINEN, M. & VÄÄTÄJÄ, H. (2010) Rewarding in open innovation communities - how to motivate members. International Journal of Entrepreneurship and Innovation Management, 11, 440-456.

ANTIKAINEN, M., VÄÄTÄJÄ, H (2008) Innovating is fun – motivations to participate in online open innovation communities. in the proceedings of the First ISPIM Innovation Symposium Singapore: Managing Innovation in a Connected World, Singapore, 14-17 December.

BISHOP, M. (2009) The Total Economic Impact of InnoCentive Challenges. Cambridge, MA, Forrester Consulting.

BONABEAU, E. (2009) Decisions 2.0: The Power of Collective Intelligence. MIT Sloan Management Review, 50, 45-+.

BUUR, J. & BAGGER, K. (1999) Replacing usability testing with user dialogue. Commun. ACM, 42, 63-66.

BUUR, J. & MATTHEWS, B. (2008) Participatory innovation. International journal of innovation management, 12, 255.

CHESBROUGH, H. W. (2003a) The era of Open Innovation. Sloan Management Review, 44, 35-41.

CHESBROUGH, H. W. (2003b) Open innovation the new imperative for creating and profiting from technology, Boston, MA, Harvard Business School Press.

CHESBROUGH, H. W. (2006) Open innovation the new imperative for creating and profiting from technology, Boston, Harvard Business School Press.

DWYER, L., AND MELLOR, R. (1991) Organizational environment, new product process activities, and project outcomes. Journal of Product Innovation Management, 8, 39-48.

EBNER, W., LEIMEISTER, J. M. & KRCMAR, H. (2009) Community engineering for innovations: the ideas competition as a method to nurture a virtual community for innovations. R&D Management, 39, 342-356.

EHN, P. & KYNG, M. (Eds.) (1987) The collective resource approach to systems design., England: Avebury, Aldershot.

EISENHARDT, K. M. (1989) Building Theories from Case Study Research. Academy of Management Review. Academy of Management.

ENKEL , E., GASSMANN, O. & CHESBROUGH, H. (2009) Open R&D and open innovation; exploring the phenomenon. R&D Management, 39, 311 - 316.

FICHTER, K. (2009) Innovation communities; the role of networks in Open Innovation. R&D Management, 39, 357-371.

FRANKE, N. & SHAH, S. (2003) How communities suport innovation activities: an exploration of assistance and sharing among end-users. Research Policy, 32, 157 - 178.

GASSMANN, O. (2006) Opening up the innovation process: towards an agenda. R&D Management, 36, 223-228.

GORDON, S., MONIDEEPA, T, ET AL. (2008) Improving the front end of innovation with information technology. Research Technology Management, 51, 50-58.

HARS, A. & OU, S. S. (2002) Working for free? Motivations for participating in open-source projects. International Journal of Electronic Commerce, 6, 25-39.

HERTEL, G., NIEDNER, S. & HERRMANN, S. (2003) Motivation of software developers in Open Source projects: an Internet-based survey of contributors to the Linux kernel. Research Policy, 32, 1159-1177.

HOLMQUIST, L. E. (2004) User-driven innovation in the future applications lab. CHI '04 extended abstracts on Human factors in computing systems. Vienna, Austria, ACM.

HOWE, J. (2006) The Rise of Crowdsourcing. Wired Magazine.

HUSTON, L., SAKKAB, N. (2006) Connect and develop: Inside Procter & Gamble's new model for innovation. Harvard business review 84, 58.

JEPPESEN, H. J. (2006) Participation and prevention when organizing shift work at company level in various European countries, Aarhus, Aarhus University Press.

LAKHANI, K. L., BOUDREAU, K. J. (2009) How to manage outside innovation. MIT Sloan Management Review, 50, 69-76.

LAKHANI, K. L., JEPPESEN, L. B., LOHSE, P. A. & PANETTA, J. A. (2006) The value of openness in scientific problem solving. Harvard Business School.

LEONARD, D. & RAYPORT, J. F. (1997) SPARK INNOVATION THROUGH EMPATHIC DESIGN. Harvard Business Review. Harvard Business School Publication Corp.

LERNER, J. & TIROLE, J. (2002) Some Simple Economics of Open Source. The Journal of Industrial Economics, 50, 197-234.

LETTL, C., HERSTATT, C. & GEMÜNDEN, H. G. (2006) User's contribution to radical innovation: Evidence from four cases in the field of medical equipment technology. . R&D Management, 36, 251-272.

MCLURE WASKO, M. & FARAJ, S. (2000) "It is what one does": why people participate and help others in electronic communities of practice. The Journal of Strategic Information Systems, 9, 155-173.

MUHDI, L., DAIBER, M., FRIESIKE, S. & BOUTELLIER, R. (2010) The Crowdsourcing process: an intermediary mediated idea generation approach in the early phase of innovation International Journal of Entrepreneurship and Innovation Management.

NOV, O. (2007) What motivates Wikipedians? Communication of the ACM, 50, 60-64.

PALS, N., STEEN, G., D., M., LANGLEY, J., D. & KORT, J. (2008) Three approaches to take the user perspective into account during new product design. International journal of innovation management 12, 275.

PISANNO, G. P., AND VERGANTI, R. (2008) Which kind of collaboration is right for you? Harvard Business Review, 86, 78-86.

ROBERTS, J. A., HANN, I. H. & SLAUGHTER, S. A. (2006) Understanding the motivations, participation, and performance of open source software developers: A longitudinal study of the Apache projects. Management Science, 52, 984-999.

ROHRACHER, H. (2005) User involvement in innovation processes: strategies and limitations from a socio-technical perspective, Verlag GmbH München-Wien.

SCHULER, D. & NAMIOKA, A. (1993) Participatory design: Principles and practices, Lawrence Erlbaum Associates.

SHAH, S. K., AND CORLEY, K.G. (2006) Building better theory by bridging the quantitative-qualitative divide. Journal of Management Studies, 43, 1821-1835.

STAKE, R. E. (1995) The art of case study research, Thousand Oaks, California [etc.], Sage Publications.

VERONA, G. & PRANDELLI, E., SAWHNEY, MOHANBIR (2006) Innovation and Virtual Environemnts; Towards Virtual Knowledge Brokers. Organization Studies.

VERWORN, B. (2009) A structural equation model of the impact of the "fuzzy front end" on the success of new product development. Research Policy, 38, 1571-1581.

VON HIPPEL, E. (1988) The sources of innovation, New York [etc.], Oxford University Press.

VON HIPPEL, E. (2006) Democratizing innovation, Cambridge, Mass., MIT Press.

VON HIPPEL, E. & VON KROGH, G. (2006) Free revealing and the private-collective model for innovation incentives R&D Management, 36, 295 - 306.

VON KROGH, G. & VON HIPPEL, E. (2006) The promise of research on open source software. Management Science, 52, 975 - 983.

WASKO, M. M. & FARAJ, S. (2000) "It is what one does": why people participate and help others in electronic communities of practice. Journal of Strategic Information Systems, 9, 155-173.

YIN, R. K. (2003) Case study research design and methods, Thousand Oaks, Sage Publications.

i want morebooks!

Buy your books fast and straightforward online - at one of world's fastest growing online book stores! Environmentally sound due to Print-on-Demand technologies.

Buy your books online at
www.get-morebooks.com

Kaufen Sie Ihre Bücher schnell und unkompliziert online – auf einer der am schnellsten wachsenden Buchhandelsplattformen weltweit! Dank Print-On-Demand umwelt- und ressourcenschonend produziert.

Bücher schneller online kaufen
www.morebooks.de

 VDM Verlagsservicegesellschaft mbH
Heinrich-Böcking-Str. 6-8
D - 66121 Saarbrücken

Telefon: +49 681 3720 174
Telefax: +49 681 3720 1749

info@vdm-vsg.de
www.vdm-vsg.de

Printed by Books on Demand GmbH, Norderstedt / Germany